Guile Is Good!

Why We Need Lawyers

John Denvir

ISBN: 1500873918
ISBN-13: 978-1500873912
Library of Congress Control Number: 2014917116
CreateSpace Independent Publishing Platform, North Charleston, SC

To

David and Audrey Fielding

Very good friends for a very long time

Contents

Acknowledgments

I wish to thank Tim Iglesias for introducing me to the concept of "professional identity," which helped me organize what otherwise might have been just some random thoughts about lawyering into a cohesive whole. Numerous friends and colleagues read earlier drafts and made helpful comments. I would especially like to thank Jim Barry, Charles Reich, Audrey Fielding, David Fielding, Alexander Auerbach, Bill Simon, Richard Sherman, and David Papke for their comments. I would also like to thank Steve Shatz, Josh Davis, Richard Leo, and Jeff Brand for helpful comments they made during my presentation of an earlier draft at a University of San Francisco School of Law faculty scholarship luncheon. I also want to thank John Shafer and Lee Ryan of the USF Law School library for their research and Internet help. My son Michael has given me a great deal of good advice on book design and publication matters. And my wife, Miriam Rokeach, has been, as always, not only an excellent editor but also a constant source of support for my intellectual efforts.

Prologue

I want to tell the story of how lawyer creativity and craft shape the world we live in. Since humor often reveals truths that more serious talk misses, let me start with a lawyer joke that encapsulates my thesis.

A university search committee is interviewing candidates for the presidency of the university. One candidate is a mathematician, another a sociologist, and the third a lawyer. At the end of each interview, one member of the committee throws in a final question: "Excuse me, but can you tell us how much is two plus two?"

The mathematician responds, "That is a really complex question, but for present purposes we can say that if you take an abstract two and add another abstract two, you get an abstract four." The questioner thanks him for his answer.

The sociologist is asked the same question at the end of her interview. She replies that "this is an empirical question that requires very careful collection and analysis of data, but roughly the range is from three to five with a mean of about four." The questioner thanks her for her answer.

As he is about to leave the interview room the lawyer is also asked, "How much is two and two?" The lawyer slowly turns around, approaches the committee, and inquires in a soft voice, "How much do you want it to be?"

The lawyer gets the job.

The punch line anticipates the thesis of this small book—the public respect and fear lawyers because they sense we use our creativity and craft (and craftiness) to shape the world. As lawyers, we should take great pride in the power our skills provide us and think carefully about how we choose to employ them.

1. The Lawyer's Genius

My goal is to present a new image or identity for the legal profession. I propose an identity that accentuates lawyerly creativity, savvy, and guile. Some members of the profession like to see themselves as philosophers, scientists, or technical experts. Critics of the profession are more likely to call us paid liars. I think the critics, although in error, make a useful contribution by highlighting the lawyer's unorthodox relationship to truth. Philosophers and scientists are trying to state the truth; you might say they are in the "truth" business. Lawyers have a more complicated relationship with truth. They are interested in truth not for its own sake but for its role in winning the case at hand. This requires them to persuade the judge and jury that their client's version of the truth is superior to that of his or her adversary. They are in the "persuasion" business. Individual lawyers concentrate on persuasion, leaving the adversary system as a whole to find the truth and do justice. But this clash of versions of the truth has important societal value. Through it, the strengths and weaknesses of the respective positions are vetted in a way that allows the best decision to emerge.

The lawyer is not a "liar" because the issue is not choosing between truth and falsity; it is arguing about what constitutes "the" truth. It's for the judge and the jury to decide what is true. By critiquing the evidence, testimony, and opposing counsel's arguments, thereby expanding the universe of possible "right" answers, the lawyer enables the decision makers to see possible answers they might have otherwise missed because of ignorance or prejudice.

Let me illustrate how lawyerly creativity, savvy, and guile work, by referencing a "lawyer" movie. In John Ford's classic 1939 film *Young Mr. Lincoln,* the young lawyer Abe Lincoln successfully defends two boys accused of a murder to which there is an alleged eyewitness. Lincoln's true genius in winning the case is not knowledge of the law or skill at cross-examination; it's his ability to invent an argument that will undermine the accuser's credibility. The accuser says he saw the murder clearly because there was a full moon that night. But Lincoln considers the possibility of a cloudy night and then researches the weather reports to discover that the almanac says it was in fact a cloudy night. This is a good example of lawyer creativity in imagining alternative narratives that might help win a case.

But Lincoln's genius does not stop here. Instead of announcing in court that it was a cloudy night, he lures the accuser into boldly testifying that the moon shone brightly. After discrediting this testimony with the evidence from the almanac, he destroys the witness's credibility not only about the weather but also about the murder. This is an example of lawyerly cunning or guile; young Lincoln disingenuously poses seemingly innocent questions that he hopes will entice the witness into lying.

Of course, Lincoln's argument is not conclusive. The almanac might have been in error, or the witness may have misremembered the weather but not the murder. But Lincoln is not engaged in a search for truth, as we might expect of a scientist or a philosopher. He wants to win the case. In so doing he has expanded the possible narratives the jury will consider, and in this case, it appears that his labors helped yield a just result.

The image of the lawyer I am proposing echoes many of the qualities that students of myth and folklore find in the character they call the "Trickster." Perhaps the Trickster best known to most Americans is Brer Rabbit, in Joel Chandler Harris's Uncle Remus tale "How Mr. Rabbit Was Too Sharp for Mr. Fox."[1] Brer Fox has finally captured Brer Rabbit and is contemplating barbecuing him for dinner. The rabbit has been sassing him for years, and he can't wait to get his revenge.

As the fox stokes the fire, Brer Rabbit starts his trickster work. He recognizes that his only chance to survive is to use the fox's desire for revenge against him. Brer Rabbit decides his best strategy is to try to persuade the fox to take the action that he himself most welcomes, but he knows he cannot make a direct request. Instead he must convince the fox that the action he actually wants is the one he purports to most fear—being thrown into the briar patch. So Brer Rabbit begs the fox to consider any one of a long list of punishments he would accept if the fox would just agree not to throw him into the briar patch. He is so convincing in describing his fears of the briar patch that the fox decides that this is the punishment he will inflict.

So the fox throws Brer Rabbit into the briar patch and waits to hear his cries of pain, only to be rewarded by the sight of the cocky rabbit sitting comfortably on a rock on the other side of the patch, taunting him with the news that he had been "bred and born in a briar patch." We see here the essence of the Trickster's talent; he uses creativity and cunning to outwit his adversary.

The Brer Rabbit stories, although written by a white author, are based on African American folk tales told by black slaves in the nineteenth century. These tales are only one example of a much larger genre of myths and folk tales from a multiplicity of cultures that tell of the exploits of a clever opportunist who confronts the world with little more than wit, audacity, and guile.[2] The protagonists in these tales are given a variety of names—Hermes (Greek), Loki (German), Krishna (Hindu), Coyote or Raven (Native American), Sindbad (Arabic), and Eshu (African)—but they all display the creative, crafty personality we identify with the Trickster.

Lewis Hyde has written a very fine book, *Trickster Makes This World: Myth, Mischief, and Art*, in which he describes the traits identified with the Trickster.[3] Hyde sees the Trickster as the incarnation of a type of creative intelligence that is driven by appetite and focused on results. Tricksters have little use for philosophy or morality; they prefer to trust their native wit in navigating a world of contingency. The usual scenario finds the Trickster hungry for something that the culture assigns to someone else. Therefore, in a sense, the Trickster's basic goal is theft—taking what society says belongs to another. Sometimes the Trickster (like Brer Rabbit) accomplishes this by means of a lie.

But Hyde points out that other times the Trickster's ruse is more complicated. The trickster Hermes in the *Homeric Hymn to Hermes* is a good example.[4] Hermes is the illegitimate child of the Greek god Zeus and the mortal Maia. His status in the world of the Gods is therefore marginal. But at birth he announces his intention to change his station in life. He does this by stealing a herd of cows belonging to the god Apollo. With great cunning, he conceals the theft from detection.

Hyde points out that Hermes's theft implicitly challenges the validity of the then-existing laws of property. By ignoring Apollo's ownership of the cows, Hermes challenges the social structure that places him in a subservient position.[5] When Apollo accuses him of theft, Hermes first lies, blithely denying any knowledge of the cows. But he does more than lie; he articulates a vision of the cultural order that legitimates his theft. He accomplishes this by singing a song to Apollo that memorializes all the gods (his references to Apollo are especially flattering), but that also includes verses that recognize Hermes himself as a full member of the divine family. Apollo, charmed by the music, the flattery, and even Hermes's audacity, cannot help but laugh, and he ends up not only pledging his friendship to Hermes but also granting Hermes lordship over the herd of cows.

The *Homeric Hymn to Hermes* shows the Trickster to be more than a winner; he is also an agent of social change. But he is not an anarchist, much less a revolutionary. He just wants to shape the social and legal landscape to his own advantage.

Hyde points out that the Trickster's ability to initiate peaceful social change provides a valuable benefit to the larger culture by keeping the ruling structure flexible and open to new ideas. Otherwise it can become brittle and eventually crack. By performing this essential social function, the scheming Trickster proves to be a cultural hero whose "lies" often turn out to be true in the long run.[6]

I believe this capacity for creativity, savvy, and cunning or guile constitutes the genius of the American lawyer. "Genius" means more than someone with a high IQ. *Webster's Dictionary* defines it as a "peculiar, distinctive, or identifying characteristic" of an institution. I fully recognize that lawyers need more than creativity, savvy, and guile to succeed. They need substantive legal knowledge and must master a variety of technical skills to do their job well, but I do believe the attribute that sets them apart from scientists, philosophers, and technical experts (as well as mathematicians and sociologists) is their ability to enlist imagination, savvy, and guile in the enterprise of persuasion.

I do not mean in any way that all tricksters are lawyers; the legal profession has no monopoly on trickster skills. Martin Luther King Jr. is a good example. We now think back on the victory of the civil rights movement as inevitable, but it didn't look that way in the spring of 1963. King had been fighting since 1955 to use the theory of nonviolence to destroy the system of apartheid in the American South. He saw nonviolence as a religious principle, but he also used it as a political tactic: "It [nonviolence] says you can struggle without hating. You can fight war without violence."[7] Nonviolent protests enabled the public to see the contrast between the Christian courage of African Americans and the violent responses of the segregationists who opposed them.

Despite many early victories, the civil rights movement had started to stall in early 1963. Police Chief Laurie Pritchett had outsmarted King during the civil rights protests in Albany, Georgia. Pritchett claimed that by arresting protesters, he was just attempting to neutrally enforce the laws against anyone who broke them. The fact that the lawbreakers were African Americans protesting segregation, and that the laws and court orders they were ignoring were unconstitutional, was irrelevant to him. Pritchett's position was that civil rights protesters, like other citizens, had to obey the law. Segregation was not the issue; respect for law was. Pritchett managed to depict civil rights protesters as common criminals. King was forced to leave Albany without winning any concessions from the segregationists.

One northern newspaper called the Albany demonstrations a "devastating loss of face" for King.[8] Supporters started to doubt King's leadership. The *New York Times* noted Pritchett's "skillful opposition."[9] Attorney General Robert Kennedy announced a "hands-off" approach to southern policing of civil rights demonstrations. Financial support from northern groups started to weaken, and even King's African American foot soldiers voiced reluctance to go to jail without any gains to justify their suffering.

Many advisors wanted to pull back and regroup, but King knew that a social movement that loses momentum soon dies. So he raised the stakes by announcing a consumer boycott and peaceful marches in Birmingham, Alabama, during Easter week of 1963.

Birmingham seemed an odd choice, since it was a bastion of segregation ruled by Police Commissioner Eugene "Bull" Conner, who was notorious for his rough treatment of union organizers and civil rights protesters. But King the trickster saw Conner's intransigence as an opportunity rather than a liability. There was a good chance that Laurie Pritchett's "professional" response to civil rights protests would not appeal to Bull Conner. King did not want violence, but if it happened he was ready to turn it to his own advantage. "If it comes, we will surface it for the world to see."[10] White violence would permit King to allow the American public to see for themselves the ugly face of racism.

The crucial decision was whether to allow thousands of black school children to participate in the civil rights marches. Some advisors said it was wrong for King to put children in harm's way, but King responded that anyone who was old enough to accept Christ was old enough to stand witness against injustice. Therefore, King's assistants organized thousands of black school children, a veritable nonviolent children's army, to march on downtown Birmingham. When Bull Conner demanded they disperse, the children responded with civil rights hymns. When Conner ordered that water cannons be turned on them, they stood their ground. When he ordered police dogs to be used to intimidate them, they refused to turn around.

All these events took place in full view of news photographers who quickly sent their films and photos to media outlets in the North. That evening, millions of Americans saw youngsters knocked off their feet by water cannons. Most memorably, one photograph showed a terrified young African American boy in his Sunday best, frozen in terror as a police dog, fangs bared, lunged at him. That picture became the nation's image of Birmingham and the segregationist South. The issue was no longer respect for law, but brutal racism. The tide had turned. A year later the landmark Civil Rights Act of 1964 was passed.

Sometimes tricksters, lawyers or laymen, use their talents to accomplish feats that we find unworthy. Advertising executive Leo Burnett is a good example. About the same time Martin Luther King Jr. was planning the civil rights campaign for Birmingham, Burnett was making his final refinements to the "Marlboro Man" campaign for Marlboro cigarettes.[11]

American tobacco companies had grown rich actually touting the health benefits of their products, but beginning in the 1950s, they were faced with the unpleasant reality of more and more scientific studies that linked smoking with cancer. Rather than accept these damning facts, "big tobacco" employed various strategies to maintain their profitable businesses. One such strategy was to claim that filters removed the health risk. Marlboro used a filter, but Burnett advised against emphasizing this fact. He wasn't worried about whether the claim was true or false; his concern was that safety claims reminded smokers of the risks smoking entailed.

Instead, he devised a very clever ad campaign to divert smokers' attention from cancer to more pleasant thoughts. Burnett's "Marlboro Man" campaign featured the image of a weathered cowhand on horseback, framed against a beautiful western landscape, enjoying a cigarette. The accompanying text was very simple: "Come to where the flavor is. Come to Marlboro Country." Tobacco advertising expert Albert Brandt says the "Marlboro cowboy suggested a mythic time, not only before the bureaucratization and urbanization of the twentieth century, but also a time of *simple* [italics in the original] pleasures, before the midcentury discovery that smoking brought risk and disease."[12] It also celebrated American independence and hostility to government telling us what to do. Just as the lone cowboy stoically faced down the elements, the smoker would conquer his or her fears, including those about the risks of smoking.

And it worked. Marlboro's manufacturer, Phillip Morris, which had been the smallest of the tobacco companies before the campaign, soon became a worldwide giant. We don't know how many people were lured to their death by Burnett's ads. But we must recognize that Burnett was no less a trickster than King. Each crafted a narrative that persuaded the public to act as he wished. So, while we cannot help but admire the trickster for his or her almost magical skills, we also must judge tricksters on how they use those skills.

I think we can see a family resemblance between the Trickster and the American lawyer. Both are activists, refusing to docilely wait for fate to play out. They intervene to tilt events in a certain direction. Both are creative artists who imagine alternatives to the status quo and devise clever strategies to bring them about. Both revel in the ambiguity of social life, seeing it as an opportunity to craft narratives that will serve their interests. This embrace of ambiguity is combined with a preference for misdirection and artifice in dealing with adversaries. And both lawyers and tricksters are more interested in concrete results than in abstract truth. They are not disinterested experts, but crafty activists scheming toward victory.

It turns out that "genius" has one additional meaning. It refers to a guardian or "tutelary spirit" that protects certain persons. In this sense I would like to propose the Trickster as the lawyer's genius, an image in which lawyers should take pride. Lawyers are creative artists of the first magnitude who are much more than their bag of tricks. They not only serve their clients' interests, but they also perform an important function by facilitating peaceful social change in societies that might otherwise lurch between rigidity and violence. But the trickster identity will also alert lawyers to the ethical responsibilities a lawyer must adopt. A trickster lawyer has to be more than just a trickster.

I realize that many lawyers will resist being identified with the scheming Trickster, preferring to see themselves as technical experts above the fray. But I think that the trickster identity not only better describes what lawyers actually do, it also should be a source of inspiration in that it shows lawyers are creative artists, not bloodless technocrats, using imagination, strategic intelligence, and cunning to shape social reality. It is true that the trickster identity also has a more cautionary message. It recognizes that lawyers are often tempted to use their skills in ethically questionable ways.

But the fact that the Trickster identity is in some ways a double-edged sword may be its greatest strength, because it mirrors the general public's ambivalence toward our profession. The public admires lawyers for our resourcefulness. Lawyers make things happen. But they also mistrust and fear the legal profession because they believe lawyers' awesome talents are often employed against the public interest. The Trickster identity reminds us that, along with the ecstasy of professional success, the lawyer must suffer the agony of deciding how to use his or her persuasive power.

2. Trickster Litigators

My goal in the following chapters is to show litigators, legal counselors, and judges exemplifying the trickster approach to the practice of law. I start with litigators. Admittedly it's the easiest case for my thesis, since trial lawyers are well known for their clever trial strategies and quickness of wit.

Gerry Spence

In the 1970s, a highly publicized lawsuit was brought against the Kerr-McGee Corporation, a company that operated a plant in Crescent, Oklahoma, which made plutonium-uranium fuel rods for use in nuclear reactors. The suit alleged that an employee at the plant, Karen Silkwood, had been contaminated by exposure to radiation in the course of her job grinding and polishing pellets that would be used in the fuel rods. Silkwood, who was also a union representative active in employee safety issues, was killed in a car crash one morning as she drove to meet a *New York Times* reporter to discuss safety issues at the plant.

Silkwood's estate was represented by Wyoming "cowboy" trial lawyer Gerry Spence. Spence's final argument to the jury in the *Silkwood v. Kerr-McGee* case is an excellent example of a trickster lawyer at work. Spence could have framed his argument in terms of logic: here is the applicable law, here are the relevant facts, and here is the conclusion you should draw.

Spence took another tack altogether. He created a multilayered narrative that sounds more like a plot for a Hollywood movie than a legal theory. He created a human drama that not only portrayed Silkwood as the fallen hero and Kerr-McGee as the callous villain, but also included a role for the jury members themselves to redeem Silkwood's death.

Phillip Meyer, in his excellent book *Storytelling for Lawyers*,[13] shows us that Spence's final argument included three independent but related narratives. The first tells us what happened at the Kerr-McGee plant in the early 1970s. Spence begins his argument by reminding the jury of the sad state of affairs that existed at the Kerr-McGee plant before Karen Silkwood arrived. He does this by summarizing the testimony of Kerr-McGee officials and former employees. Remember that Spence had two and a half months of testimony to choose from in crafting his story. Knowing that an emotionally moving story needs a villain as much as it needs a hero, he chose testimony that tended to stress the opposition be-tween the "evil" corporation and the "innocent" workers it harmed.

Mr. Utnage, the man who designed the plant, is a good example of a "company" witness. Here is Spence's description of Mr. Ut-nage.

> I want to talk about the design of the plant very quickly. It was designed by Mr. Utnage. He never designed any kind of plant...And I confronted him with scores of prob-lems—you remember those 574 reports of contaminations—they were that thick (*indicating*), in two volumes...I asked him about a leak detection system. "We do not need a leak detection system," he said. "We can see it. We can see it." Here is the man who told you that as long as you can't see it, you're safe. And we know that the amount of plutonium, a half of a gram of pluto-

nium, will contaminate the whole state of Oklahoma, and you can't see it…He sat there on the stand under his oath and looked at every one of you under his oath and he said that plutonium has never been known to cause cancer. Well, now he either lied, or he bought the company lie and didn't know. But he was the man who designed the plant. You wouldn't have to design a very good plant if you didn't think plutonium caused cancer, it wouldn't bother you. You wouldn't work very hard. There wouldn't be much to worry about.[14]

Spence also reminds the jury of "young Apperson," who he sees as one of the "innocent" workers duped by Kerr-McGee:

Do you remember young Apperson sitting there (*indicating*)? You remember his open face—I liked him a lot—an open, honest boy—blond curly hair—you remember him, two and a half months ago. He said "thirty percent of the pipes were not welded when I came, when the plant was opened. Thirty percent of the pipes were welded after the plant was in operation, and I was there, and I saw those old welds." And he wasn't a certified welder himself, and he was teaching people in an hour or two to be welders themselves—not a certified welder on the job. "There were things leaking everywhere," he said. You remember how he was describing how he was there welding the pipe and they jerked the oxygen out, and he had to gasp for air—the contamination—to survive the moment?[15]

The stage is now set for the hero's entrance. Spence wants the jury to know two things about Karen Silkwood: she was an "ordinary" person much like themselves, but she was also a "special" person, because she "cared."

> She was a happy child, a good child, she was correctly raised by the church, and she loved church, and she was a scholarship student, and she was a chemistry major. She was bright, she could understand. But, more than anything else, she cared. At that corporation plant there was some-body who cared, and it was Karen Silkwood. Somebody who cared a lot about others.[16]

Spence then played tape recordings of Silkwood's voice for the jury, as she described her activities at the plant.

> Ah, in the laboratory we got eighteen- and nineteen-year-old boys, you know, twenty and twenty-one, I mean, and they didn't have the schooling so they don't understand what radiation is. They don't understand...they don't understand.[17]

Finally Spence answers what he sees as the crucial question that faces the jury—"who was Karen Silkwood?"

> Who was she? I say she was a prophet, an ordinary woman who cared, and could understand, doesn't have to be anything other than an ordinary woman who cared and understood in order to be a prophet. I don't mean she's anything, you know, biblical—I mean, she was an ordi-nary person who cared, and she prophesied this way: "If there is something going on"—this is an actual quote—"If there is something going on, we're going to be susceptible to cancer, and we're not going to know about it for years." She says this to you, ladies and gentlemen. "Something has to be done."[18]

Both Spence and the jury knew that Silkwood died in a car crash on her way to meet a *New York Times* reporter with the express purpose of getting something done.

Spence's second narrative moves from the events that precipitated the trial to what transpired at the trial itself. He spends relatively little time reviewing the facts necessary to his theory of the case, because he knows the applicable law favors him. The court had decided that the case was one of "strict liability": if Kerr-McGee caused Silkwood's contamination, it was legally liable, even if it could show it was not negligent in doing so. Spence reduces the law to a catchy phrase: "If the lion (the plutonium) got away, Kerr-McGee (the owner of the plutonium) must pay."

That said, there was only one legal theory that could save Kerr-McGee. If Kerr-McGee could prove that Silkwood voluntarily contaminated herself, it would provide a winning affirmative defense to her claim. Unfortunately, from Kerr-McGee's perspective, there was no hard evidence to show such voluntary contamination. But the defense team still decided to give it a try by pointing out that there was radioactive material found in Silkwood's apartment, which she might have smuggled out of the plant. But how would she smuggle it out? In his opening statement to the jury, Kerr-McGee's chief attorney, William Paul, had tried to suggest an answer to that question by pantomiming Silkwood putting the plutonium into her jacket pocket. However, that still left the question of motive. Why would a young, healthy woman, aware of the danger of contact with plutonium, contaminate herself? The only theory Kerr-McGee could offer was that it was an act of revenge against Kerr-McGee.

Law is often a game of wits. Two lawyers meet, each trying to outsmart the other. Kerr-McGee's counsel had decided to base his defense on a personal attack on Karen Silkwood. But Spence immediately recognized that, in doing so, Paul had opened up two opportunities for Spence to add to his portrait of the villainous corporation.

First, he can point out that Mr. Paul is attacking the reputation of a "good" girl who is not alive to defend herself. And second, since Mr. Paul has had to resort to speculation and innuendo to make his case that Silkwood intentionally exposed herself to radiation as an act of revenge against the corporation, Spence can claim the right to speculate himself about the answer to a question he knows is on the jury's mind. How did Karen Silkwood die?

> Mr. Paul...stood up here and pointed his finger toward Karen Silkwood...Mr. Paul doesn't have the right to come into court and say "I think this happened" and "I think *that* happened."...And to take a whole series of unrelated events and put them together...and to mislead you...But if Mr. Paul wants to play guess-um—that is, point the finger...I am willing to play that game. But, when I do it, I want you to know it isn't right, because I can't prove *that* any more than they can prove it.[19]

After this ritualistic admission that he has no proof to support his charges, Spence tells the story he really wants the jury to hear, the one that is not "legally" relevant—the story of who killed Karen Silkwood. Did Kerr-McGee have good reason to see Silkwood dead?

> I can give you motive. What was the motive for them to do that? She was a troublemaker. She was doing union negotiations. She was on her way—she was gathering documents—every day in that union, everybody in that company, everybody in management knew that...She knew too much. What would she do if she had gotten to

18

the *New York Times*?[20]

One might ask why Spence was so interested in the question of how Silkwood died, since it was formally not an issue in the case. Kerr-McGee was liable for her contamination whether or not they were involved in her death. But Spence knew that while the circumstances of her death were not "legally" relevant, how the jury pictured Silkwood's death would play a large role in their determination of damages, especially exemplary or (as they are commonly called) "punitive" damages. By this point in the trial, everyone must know that the only issue in doubt is the amount of damages the jury will award.

Now the stage is set for the concluding portion of Spence's narrative. Let's review what he has set out up to this point. In the first narrative, Spence introduces the villain, Kerr-McGee, a corporation that, at a minimum, is careless in its safety standards and insensitive to the health dangers its innocent employees face. Spence also introduces the hero, Karen Silkwood. Karen is a "good girl" and an "ordinary person," but also someone who "cares about people." When she discovers that Kerr-McGee has not informed the "young boys" of the dangers they face, she decides "something has to be done." This transforms her from ordinary bystander to hero. She compiles evidence to show to a *New York Times* reporter, but is mysteriously killed in a car crash shortly before the scheduled meeting.

Spence then tells the story of the trial itself. Spence uses Kerr-McGee's attempt to blame Silkwood for her own contamination as a springboard to add to his own story of villainous corporation versus courageous hero. He suggests to the jury that there is good reason to believe that Silkwood was murdered by Kerr-McGee because the corporation feared what would happen if she ever did talk to that reporter.

Now we come to the third and concluding narrative. Here, the time is no longer the past, and the hero is no longer only Karen Silkwood. The time is the present and another hero appears—the jury, "ordinary" citizens who, like Karen, "care." They now have the opportunity to make sure that Karen's death was not in vain. They can redeem Karen's death by delivering an award that will make Kerr-McGee pay for her death and make the nuclear industry take action to prevent future disasters.

I think it is worthwhile here to point out the constantly shifting roles that Spence plays in the trial. Sometimes he plays the role of law-explainer. ("If the lion got away, Kerr-McGee must pay.") Other times he functions as an informal witness who tells the jury of possibilities that are emotionally powerful, even if unproven or legally irrelevant. Now, in the third narrative, he becomes the jury's counselor, who understands their hopes and fears and helps them do what they know in their hearts is right. In fact, by the end of his plea, Spence is no longer addressing the jury as "you." He speaks about the noble task "we" must accomplish.

But first he starts his final plea, not with a call for justice, but a meditation about fear, his fear and the jury's fear.

> I, during the recess, wondered whether there is enough in all of us to do what we have to do. I'm afraid—I'm afraid of two things: I am afraid you have been worn out, and there might not be enough left in you to hear, even if you try, and I know that you will try, but I know you are exhausted; and I've been afraid there isn't enough left in me, that my mind is not clear and sharp now, and that I can't say the things I need to say, and yet it has to be done, and it has to be done well...And this is the last time that anyone will speak for Karen Silkwood. And when your verdict comes out, it will be the last time anybody

will have the opportunity that you have, and it is so important that we have the strength and the power to do what we need to do...You know history has always at crucial times reached down to the masses and picked ordinary people and gave ordinary people extraordinary power. [21]

Then suddenly his fear turns into righteous anger.

I want to tell you something about myself. I have been in courtrooms in Wyoming, little old towns in Wyoming, five thousand there. I grew up in Riverton, Wyoming, five thousand people there—Dubois, Rock Springs. I've been all over. I've been the county attorney, and prosecuted murderers—eight years I was a prosecutor—and I prosecuted murderers and thieves, and drunk and crazy people, and I've sued careless corporations in my life, and I want to tell you I have never seen a company who represented to the workers that the workers were cheated out of their lives. These people that were in charge knew of plutonium. They knew what alpha particles did. They hid the facts, and they confused the facts, and they tried to confuse you, and they tried to cover it...You and I know what it was all about. It was about a lousy $3.50 dollar-an-hour job. And if those people knew that they were going to die from cancer thirty or forty years later, would they have gone to work? The misrepresentations stole their lives. It's sickening. It's willful. It's callous...[22]

And then he tells the jury that it is not only their responsibility, but also their privilege, to write the proper ending to the Karen Silkwood story.

What is this case about? It's about Karen Silkwood, who

was a brave, ordinary woman who did care. And she had something to tell the world, and she tried to tell the world. What was it that Karen Silkwood tried tell the world? That has been left for us to say now. It's for you the jury to say for her. What was she trying to tell the world?

I think she would say, "Brothers and sisters, they were just eighteen- and nineteen-year-olds. They didn't understand. There wasn't any training. They kept the dangers a secret. They covered it with word games and number games..." And she would say "Friends, it has to stop here today. It has to stop in Oklahoma City today."[23]

The lawyer spoke, and the jury acted. After deliberations the jury awarded the Silkwood estate $500,000 compensatory damages for personal injury; $5,000 compensatory damages for property damage; and $10 million for exemplary, or punitive, damages.

Charles Houston and Thurgood Marshall

Gerry Spence, with his Stetson hat, buckskin sports coat, and flowing silver hair, seemed a trickster lawyer directly from Central Casting. But other lawyers show themselves to be just as clever as Spence, even if they exhibit a more conservative courtroom style. Charles Houston and Thurgood Marshall were two such lawyers.

In 1930, the young lawyers at the National Association for the Advancement of Colored People (NAACP) faced a problem very similar to the one Martin Luther King Jr. faced thirty years later—how, with scarce resources, to fight racial segregation in the South. It turned out that their solution to that problem helped make King's later victory possible. The NAACP first decided to focus on how to end segregation in state public schools, because they saw that the inferior education it caused was the primary obstacle to economic and social advancement for southern blacks.

After 250 years of slavery, blacks had finally been given their legal freedom after the Civil War, but, for the vast majority, life had not dramatically changed in terms of economic or social status. A major cause of this unhappy situation was the South's adoption of Jim Crow laws in the late nineteenth century, laws that created what can only be described as a racial class system.

Worse yet, the US Supreme Court, in the case of *Plessy v. Ferguson*,[24] had approved those laws as consistent with the Fourteenth Amendment's promise of "equal protection of the laws." The *Plessy* case was decided in 1896 and applied only to segregated seating in railroad cars, but the court had extended it to public education soon thereafter and had reaffirmed that position as late as 1927. Second-class education threatened to perpetuate second-class citizenship. African American children had no chance to advance themselves without a good education and no chance of a good education in the underfinanced segregated school systems in place in the South.

The young lawyers at the NAACP, led by Charles Houston, knew *Plessy* had to be attacked, but how to do so was a difficult problem. They had three options. One option was filing lawsuits that demanded that the Supreme Court reverse the *Plessy* decision outright. This made good sense from the perspective of logic, but none from the perspective of judicial politics. There was zero chance that the conservative Supreme Court of the early 1930s would overturn *Plessy*. Therefore, many argued for the second strategy, which was that African Americans should give up on the courts and concentrate on other avenues of reform.

But, the NAACP chose a third strategy, one that culminated twenty-four years later in the Supreme Court's unanimous ruling in *Brown v. Board of Education*,[25] which found that segregated schools violated the Fourteenth Amendment's equal protection clause.

Richard Kluger has eloquently told the story of the NAACP's march to victory in his classic book *Simple Justice*.[26] It's a story in which trickster lawyers play a large role. The NAACP legal team, headed first by Charles Houston and later by Thurgood Marshall, recognized there was more than one way to attack *Plessy*. They chose a less direct strategy than challenging the constitutionality of segregated schools outright. Instead, and more effectively, they decided to use the case's own language against it.

The *Plessy* opinion had ruled that facilities segregated by race but otherwise equal in quality were constitutionally acceptable. But everyone knew that the equality in quality was a myth. South Carolina was not atypical in spending ten dollars on educating each white child for every dollar it spent educating black children. So the NAACP decided not to attack the constitutionality of segregation in theory, but only the unequal way the system was administered.

This would be more palatable to the courts, since it theoretically did not challenge the idea of segregation itself. And Houston and Marshall saw how a modest theory might work dramatic changes in the long run. They knew that if the courts forced the South to actually provide two educational systems of equal quality, the expense would be prohibitive. Eventually the South would have to accept a single integrated school system for economic reasons, even if they opposed it on ideological grounds. Here we see how an understanding of how the system really operates can generate a sophisticated litigation strategy.

The NAACP made a second clever tactical decision about the scope of the early cases. The NAACP knew the heart of the problem was segregation at the grade school and high school levels.

This was the segregation that limited the economic possibilities for most blacks. But they also knew judges would be reluctant to act at these levels. Not only was there the expense involved, but lawsuits involving grade schools and high schools raised the fear of the racial mixing of young children, an incendiary topic in the South.

So the NAACP started by challenging segregation at the professional and graduate school levels. Not only was the expense involved smaller, but the students involved were adults. The NAACP lawyers saw another value in these modest attempts. Victories in these cases would start building a body of precedent that might eventually undermine the *Plessy* decision itself. If a segregated law school is found to be unconstitutional, the question logically arises of why segregation is any more acceptable at the high school and grade school levels. The NAACP lawyers had the vision to see how these "small" victories might play out in the long run.

The lawsuits also aimed to perform political and legal functions. If successful, they would show African Americans that victory over segregation was indeed possible. And, even if unsuccessful, they operated as a form of political theatre that allowed the NAACP to instruct the courts, the press, and the public on the irrationality and cruelty of segregation.

For instance, in *McLaurin v. Oklahoma State Regents*,[27] the state attempted to fulfill its duties under the equal protection clause by accepting a black student but still maintaining a segregated graduate school of education. This led to a bizarre situation Kluger describes well.

> And so the sixty-eight-year-old George McLaurin was made to sit at a desk by himself in an anteroom outside the regular classrooms where his course work was given. In the library he was assigned to a segregated desk behind

half a carload of newspapers. In the cafeteria he was required to eat in a dingy alcove and at a different hour from the whites.[28]

The NAACP knew fair-minded judges would be reluctant to approve such schemes. Even if they ruled against the NAACP, the public would see the true face of segregation.

This strategy started paying dividends by the 1940s. The Supreme Court had ruled in several cases that states would have to build truly equal professional and graduate schools for blacks or admit them as equals to existing schools.[29] This clearly was progress; segregation was dead at the highest level of education. But it was slow progress, because it allowed generation after generation of Southern black children to grow up in segregated elementary and high schools.

So Thurgood Marshall decided to raise the ante. He meant to challenge the constitutionality of segregated elementary and high schools no matter how equally they were funded. The evil was not just unequal funds, but segregation itself. Segregation had to end at all levels of public education.

Here another tactical problem arose. How was Marshall going to prove that segregation itself, not the unequal facilities, caused the equal protection violation? How was he going to impress on white judges how segregation harmed black children? The answer came from a young black psychologist and his set of dolls. The psychologist Kenneth Clarke had developed a test in which African American children between the ages of three and seven were shown four toy dolls. The dolls were identical except that two were white and two were black. Clarke would then ask each child to hand the "nice" doll to him. Most of the black children would hand him a white doll. This was even true of children as young as three years old.[30] Here was dramatic evidence of how black children's self-image was affected by being raised in a racist culture.

But many of Marshall's advisors argued against using Clarke's doll test in court. They counseled that judges would not be impressed by "social science" evidence. In addition, it was hard to show a direct connection between those tests and the legal issue of the effects of segregated schools on black children. In fact, Clarke had found that black children in the (nominally) unsegregated schools in the North actually chose the white doll more frequently than black children attending segregated schools in the South.

But Marshall realized that the emotional impact of the tests outweighed technical arguments about their relevance. These tests worked on a visceral level the way other evidence could not. It is impossible not to feel compassion for the innocent black children who choose the white doll over one of their own skin color. Even a judge who sees its "legal" weakness cannot but feel the emotional impact. Marshall's faith in Clarke's doll tests was rewarded when Chief Justice Earl Warren stated in the *Brown* opinion that "segregation with the sanction of law has a tendency to [retard] the educational and emotional development of negro children" and cited social science evidence, including Clarke's tests, to support that conclusion.[31]

When the NAACP cases challenging segregated schools finally reached the Supreme Court in 1952, they were greeted by a court that was divided on a number of issues, including the constitutionality of segregated schools. Several justices were ready to strike down segregation, others were reluctant to do so, and still others were undecided on what to do. The court decided to buy time by asking all the parties to answer a series of narrow questions framed by the court to help the justices reach a decision.

The first question put the NAACP in a quandary. It read, "What evidence is there that the Congress which submitted and the legislatures…which ratified the Fourteenth Amendment contemplated…that it would abolish segregation in public schools?"[32]

Did the framers of the Fourteenth Amendment specifically intend to abolish segregated schools? This question was troublesome because the NAACP's exhaustive research of the historical records showed little evidence of such intent.[33] In fact, segregated schools were common both in the North and South at the time the Fourteenth Amendment was passed and ratified. How were the NAACP lawyers to respond to a question if the only honest answer cast doubt on the strength of their case?

Here the trickster enters. If you don't like the question asked, answer one you like better. The NAACP's brief in reply would ignore the question of Congress's intent with regard to segregated schools and focus on the larger historical fact—the humanitarianism and social idealism that fueled the Abolitionist movement, which was the ideological force behind the Fourteenth Amendment's passage.

But there were troublesome arguments that could not be ignored. One was the fact that John Bingham, the author of the Fourteenth Amendment, had made a speech in which he agreed to remove a provision banning "discrimination" from the Civil Rights Act of 1866. He acted in response to complaints that the "no discrimination" language in the proposed act would apply to segregated schools. Since scholars agreed that the Fourteenth Amendment was passed in order to legitimate the Civil Rights Act of 1866, it seemed contradictory to argue that the Amendment banned practices that the Civil Rights Act permitted. The NAACP appeared trapped.

But Thurgood Marshall insisted there must be an argument that would square Bingham's comments with the broad interpretation of the text of the Fourteenth Amendment, which he needed. Alfred Kelly, a historian working with the NAACP, set out the task the NAACP lawyers and their historian advisors faced. "It was not that we were formulating lies; there was nothing as crude and naïve as that. But we were using facts, emphasizing facts, bearing down on facts in a way to do what Marshall said we had to do..."[34] They had to find a way to place a plausible gloss on Bingham's comments that would support the NAACP's broad reading of the Fourteenth Amendment.

Then Kelly hit upon it ("It was like lightning breaking through."[35]): the abolitionist Bingham was willing to forego a "no discrimination" clause in the Civil Rights Act because he believed the language of the Fourteenth Amendment made it unnecessary. The Amendment's intent was not only to ratify the Civil Rights Act but to go beyond the Act to provide "equal protection of the laws" which forbade racial discrimination. With Kelly's interpretation, Bingham's comments no longer undercut the NAACP's view of the Fourteenth Amendment; they supported it.

Necessity was indeed the mother of this legal invention. Kelly had his insight only because the NAACP litigation strategy needed it. But upon reflection, he came to believe that it was indeed the correct one. And not only was the NAACP's larger theory of the humanitarian purposes of the Fourteenth Amendment adopted by the Supreme Court in the *Brown* case, but it also inspired the many later decisions of the Supreme Court since *Brown* that have extended the "no arbitrary discrimination" principle of the equal protection clause to other areas like discrimination against women and gays, groups that clearly were not contemplated as beneficiaries of the Amendment by its authors.[36] The NAACP's version of the meaning of the Fourteenth Amendment turned out to be true.

Eliot Spitzer

Trickster lawyers like Gerry Spence and Thurgood Marshall play the role of supplicant. Like Brer Rabbit, they use imagination and cunning to persuade the powerful to do their bidding. Eliot Spitzer was a different type of trickster lawyer, one who comes, not as a humble supplicant, but as an avenging angel.

Whether the moguls of Wall Street feared anyone in 1998 is open to question. Perhaps they had some trepidation about Congress and the Securities and Exchange Commission (SEC), but certainly they had little concern about the office of the Attorney General of the State of New York. To Wall Street titans, the New York attorney general was just a local politician, while they were, in Tom Wolfe's famous phrase, "masters of the universe."

That all changed in 1998, when Eliot Spitzer was narrowly elected to the office of New York State Attorney General.[37] Spitzer's style differed from that of Gerry Spence and Thurgood Marshall. He was not a spellbinding orator like Spence, nor did he attempt to appeal to high ideals like Marshall. He was a brash opportunist, ready to use highly publicized cases to promote the public interest while at the same time advancing his own political career. Yet Spitzer's ambition, daring, and toughness forced Wall Street to answer for unconscionable practices by which they had profited for years. Sometimes it takes more than charm to effect change.

Spitzer appeared to be an unlikely populist reformer. He came from a wealthy New York family, had attended elite schools, and started his legal career at one of Wall Street's most prestigious law firms. But Spitzer also believed that our financial system only worked if small investors were protected from the greed of large corporations and that it was his job as attorney general to provide that protection.

The trickster lawyer often finds new uses for old laws. For Spitzer, the old law was New York's Martin Act. When passed in the 1920s, the Martin Act had been a toothless protection against financial fraud, but later amendments to the law had given the state attorney general expansive powers to investigate and prosecute financial fraud. Prior attorneys general had pretty much ignored Wall Street because they believed it was already covered by the SEC. But Spitzer took a more aggressive view of his jurisdiction.

His strategy was to sniff out a potential misuse of financial power and then use his authority under the Martin Act to issue subpoenas requiring Wall Street firms to hand over relevant records. If those records showed illegal conduct, he approached the potential defendant with a demand for a settlement that admitted liability and promised structural reform. Spitzer left open the question of whether he would file civil or criminal charges. Criminal charges were harder to prove, but even the possibility of a criminal case against a corporation or its senior executives pressured the corporation to accept a settlement to avoid the disastrous publicity that would affect the corporation's stock price.

One of Spitzer's attorneys came to him with a news story reporting the interesting fact that a study of eight thousand stock reports, issued by stock analysts at brokerage houses that also provided investment banking services, showed only twenty-nine that recommended a "sell" of the stock analyzed. What might explain why these firms were so optimistic about the value of the stocks of 99.6 percent of the companies they analyzed? One of Spitzer's bright young lawyers had a possible explanation. Most large Wall Street financial firms had both investment and brokerage sides of their business. The investment side made millions of dollars by handling the initial stock offerings of new companies. One inducement these firms could offer to secure the investment banking business of these companies would be a promise that the stock analysts on the brokerage side of the bank would provide an optimistic report on the value of the new company's shares.

Spitzer's office served a subpoena on the giant Merrill Lynch, asking for its records relating to a rare downgrade of a stock by the firm's star analyst Henry Blodgett. The subpoenas produced e-mails that indicated Blodgett had given a "buy" recommendation for the stock of a company that Merrill Lynch management hoped would use their investment banking services, and then downgraded the stock in a report issued the day that company decided not to use Merrill for its stock offering.

Spitzer had a strong case against Blodgett, but he refused to stop there. He hoped to show that it was not just one "bad" analyst, but that the entire game was rigged against people who relied on in-house stock recommendations from financial firms active in investment banking. So he sent out more subpoenas, and more incriminating e-mails came back.

At this point, Merrill Lynch and its attorneys started to take Spitzer seriously. They came to a meeting at his office with the goal of explaining why neither Blodgett nor Merrill Lynch had broken any law. They chose an informal meeting, because this was the way the SEC had handled similar cases, showing potential defendants a good deal of courtesy. The Merrill Lynch attorneys expected similar courtesy from Spitzer, but they had a surprise coming. His reply was short and to the point: "I'm here to talk about remedies, not liability."[38] There would be no discussion of Merrill's possible innocence.

After attempting to divert the case by various means, Merrill Lynch eventually agreed to discuss a settlement admitting liability. They were willing to pay a fine, but they wanted the incriminating e-mails to be sealed. Again, this was not an unusual request; SEC settlements often included such confidentiality provisions. Spitzer's response, however, was curt and negative: "In a case of structural impact, where there is an underlying practice that needs to be reformed, the only way to do that is to lay out the evidence."[39]

When Merrill refused his harsh settlement offer on a Thursday, Spitzer told his team: "I want to file on Monday." And it was no conventional lawsuit. Spitzer's lawyers had found a provision in the Martin Act that allowed them to file the lawsuit "ex parte"— the defendants were not allowed to appear before the judge. Their complaint requested the judge to issue an order that required Merrill Lynch to tell its customers about conflicts of interest that could bias its research.

As soon as the requested relief was granted and the court hearing ended, the press conference began. Spitzer told the assembled reporters that the case represented a "shocking betrayal of trust by one of Wall Street's most trusted names."[40] Merrill's lawyers were dumbfounded when they heard about the judge's order. "We were lulled into thinking we were still in negotiations. They basically snuck behind our backs into court."[41]

When Merrill continued to stall, Spitzer threatened to use the Martin Act's provisions permitting him to bring top Merrill executives into court for public testimony about their research practices. And there was always the possibility of a criminal complaint. Merrill's lawyers told its chief executive, David Komansky, they believed they could successfully defend Blodgett and the firm against a fraud complaint. But Komansky had had enough.

Merrill's stock price had dropped 20 percent since Spitzer's filing. He decided to settle. In the final settlement Merrill agreed to pay a $100 million penalty, issue a statement of contrition, and take steps to insulate its analysts from management pressures.

But Eliot Spitzer was just getting started. The publicity from the Merrill Lynch settlement caused unhappy Wall Street employees to tip off Spitzer about other illegal schemes that allowed insiders to profit at the expense of ordinary investors. One such scheme involved the hedge fund Canary Capital Management. Canary traded only in the shares of mutual funds, timing its purchases to take advantage of short term fluctuations in price. It was much easier to win at this game if you could purchase stock in a fund after stock exchange trading hours had closed, because you could factor in the effects of news released after hours. But such "late trades" were illegal. Canary found that mutual fund executives might ignore the ban on late trading if they were offered a financial incentive. Canary found the right incentive. The fee paid to the management by a fund was a percentage of the total assets of the fund at the end of each reporting period. If a mutual fund operated by Bank of America would allow Canary to make late trades, Canary promised to reciprocate by parking large amounts of money in the Bank of America fund at the end of each reporting period. Both companies would profit, but the small investors in the fund would lose—both because late trades are more expensive to execute, and because investors would be paying an artificially inflated fee to the mutual fund management.

Spitzer immediately saw that the practice could be a violation of the Martin Act, sent out the necessary subpoenas, and confronted Canary with the incriminating e-mails the subpoenas yielded. Aware of the financial price that Merrill Lynch had paid for initially fighting Spitzer, Canary quickly agreed to a settlement.

Spitzer then immediately called a press conference in which he used Canary's admissions as evidence that there was a larger structural dysfunction in the mutual fund industry. "The mutual-fund industry works on a double standard. Certain companies and individuals have been allowed to manipulate the system..."[42] The resulting publicity persuaded the SEC, with its much greater investigatory resources, to bring its own cases against giant mutual funds. And Spitzer could start looking for new prey.

Some lawyers would have been satisfied with these concrete successes, but Spitzer was inspired to formulate a new theory of federalism. Conservative Republican politicians had long used the term "federalism" to rein in what they saw as overeager regulation of business by Democratic presidents. It was a code word for less governmental regulation. But Spitzer now argued that his success showed that federalism should lead to more regulation, if only states would take their responsibility to protect their citizens seriously. Now big business had two sets of regulators to satisfy: state and federal teams that could either cooperate or challenge each other to greater efforts. I think this is a good example of a trickster lawyer re-describing the world in a new way, and, in so doing, expanding the range of alternatives open to society in controlling the financial system.

And, of course, all the resulting publicity was only good news for Elliot Spitzer the politician. In fact, he was elected governor of New York in 2006 by a landslide margin. People were comparing him to the two Roosevelts who had moved from the governorship of New York to the White House.

John Denvir

3. Trickster Counselors

It is perhaps not surprising that litigators often fit the trickster profile. Litigators are seen as the extroverted showmen of the legal profession, and we have come to expect outsized antics from them. But many readers may find it difficult to think of the lawyer-counselor as a trickster. We see lawyers who advise clients as cautious and conservative, two adjectives seldom applied to tricksters. Yet I think we will see a trickster element in the work of the best legal counselors. They too use imagination, savvy, and cunning to guide their clients through choppy legal waters.

Samuel C. T. Dodd

One good example of the counselor trickster is John D. Rockefeller's lawyer, Samuel C. T. Dodd. Rockefeller's business's transformation from a small partnership engaged in the wholesale trade of commodities like meat and grain into the world's most powerful corporation might well be the iconic story of American capitalism, and Samuel C. T. Dodd played an important role in that story.[43] By the 1880s, Rockefeller had used the Ohio-chartered Standard Oil Company to create a virtual monopoly on the refining and transportation of oil in the United States. But this success created serious legal problems for Standard Oil. Standard Oil, and the companies it owned or controlled, owned property in many states. Each of those states had the power to tax the corporation, and some (such as Pennsylvania) based taxation on total corporate wealth instead of the value of land the corporation owned within the state. This made Standard Oil vulnerable to multiple states claiming taxes based on the corporation's total wealth. Moreover, Standard Oil's Ohio corporate charter did not authorize it to own property outside the state, a requirement the corporation was clearly violating.

The question of how Standard Oil could operate as a nationwide business within the narrow legal scheme of state corporate regulation was placed in Dodd's hands. Dodd was not a free-enterprise ideologue; before taking on Standard Oil as a client, he had opposed some of its most controversial tactics. But he was a consummate legal professional. His client had a problem and his job was to solve it. And luckily for Rockefeller, Dodd was a wizard at contriving legal structures that obeyed the letter but circumvented the spirit of constricting laws.

How could Rockefeller run a national operation like Standard Oil within the legal constrictions of narrow state corporation laws (like Ohio's) and greedy state taxing schemes (like Pennsylvania's)? Dodd came up with the answer, a plan that was legal but still gave Rockefeller the autonomy he needed. First, Dodd suggested that separate Standard Oil corporations be set up in all the states where Standard Oil owned property. Then there would be a swap between the local corporations so that each corporation only owned property in the state of its incorporation. That not only put all the corporations in compliance with charter requirements like Ohio's, which did not permit them to own property out of state, but it also prevented states from attempting to use Standard Oil's presence within their borders to justify taxing the wealth of the whole Standard Oil operation. Now each corporation only owned property in its own state.

But this scheme did not solve the problem of how Rockefeller could run a national operation from a base of forty legally independent companies. Dodd solved that problem too, using the venerable legal doctrine of trust. A properly structured trust agreement would not only provide the flexibility Rockefeller needed, but since it was a private agreement between shareholders, it would be beyond the scope of state corporation laws.

Here is how it worked. There were only forty-one investors in the Standard Oil companies, all of them connected with Rockefeller. Each of them deeded their shares in all the respective companies to a trust supervised by nine trustees, all Rockefeller loyalists. In return, the trust gave each of the investors a certificate of trust that guaranteed payment of a pro rata share of the dividends declared by each of the Standard Oil companies. The trustees were given power to elect the boards of the legally independent companies. The trustees were thus the de facto directors of a functional national corporation, but answerable to no government.

Dodd had created an imaginative construct that gave Rockefeller all the power he wanted, but did so within the operative legal framework. He had obeyed the letter of existing law but eluded its spirit. While his tactics were different from those of Gerry Spence, I think we can see that Dodd exhibited the same combination of creativity and cunning we identify with the trickster.

Martin Lipton

Corporate lawyers today are no less clever than their nineteenth-century forerunners. Take, for instance, Martin Lipton of Wachtell, Lipton, Rosen, and Katz.[44] Lipton's firm is now considered by many to be the most prestigious corporate law firm in the world. But his future did not seem so promising when he graduated from

NYU Law School in the 1950s. It wasn't that Lipton was not bright; he had been editor in chief of the school's law review. But as late as the 1950s, even brilliant young Jewish lawyers were unable to find employment with the prestigious Wall Street firms that represented the cream of corporate America.

So Lipton and three classmates started their own firm and took the clients that came to them. Often these cases involved legal issues that that the more established firms would rather not handle. One such type of lawsuit involved "unfriendly" takeover bids for control of large corporations. The prestigious firms shared their corporate clients' view that such corporate "raids" were a breach of gentlemanly conduct. But new firms like Wachtell, Lipton, Rosen, and Katz were happy to get the business. Lipton himself often represented the aggressor in these battles, but he became even more famous as an architect of defenses for corporations that were the targets of such unfriendly takeovers.

The late 1970s and early 1980s were the era of the "corporate raider." A raider like T. Boone Pickens's Mesa Petroleum would pick a target and quietly amass a quantity of shares of that corporation's stock. The plan was to choose a company whose stock was selling at a low price that undervalued the corporation's assets. Then the raider would announce an offer to buy the number of shares necessary to control the corporation, with a promise to buy the remaining shares at a later date. The offer would include a price for the shares well above their market value and a very short deadline for acceptance. Shareholders had to agree quickly to sell their shares or risk being left out of the deal. Raiders employed this "quick strike" strategy in order to gain control of the corporation before its board of directors could mount an effective counterattack.

Unfortunately for the target corporations, there were few effective tools for a corporation's management to employ in defending against a hostile takeover. They could raise antitrust concerns by attempting to persuade the Justice Department that the raiding corporation and its target engaged in the same businesses, or they could sue under state "antitakeover" statutes to enjoin the hostile offer. These approaches had some success in the early years, but they eventually became empty threats as antitrust laws were given less stringent interpretations by the US Supreme Court and state antitakeover statutes were ruled unconstitutional.

The only viable options left to the target corporation's board seemed to be to buy the raider's stock at a premium, or to find a "white knight"—a "friendly" corporation that would make an offer for control of the company more to the incumbent management's liking. The first option was not only very expensive—the raider would expect a large premium for its shares—but also amounted to submitting to extortion. The "white knight" route was also unattractive because it meant giving up control of the corporation. Moreover, there was no guarantee that a corporation that at first appeared to be friendly would remain so as time went on.

So corporate boards had a problem and, like John D. Rockefeller before them, they brought their problem to a lawyer. Some corporate targets sought the advice of Martin Lipton. His response was to invent a proactive defense tactic that came to be called the "poison pill." Lipton's strategy was to stop hostile offers before they were made by convincing the potential raider that a hostile offer would trigger consequences the raider would find most unpalatable (hence the name "poison pill").

There are many versions of the poison pill defense, but a simple example will provide the essence of the strategy. Consider a corporation that has 1,000,000 outstanding shares of stock and an undervalued stock price. It knows it is a potential takeover target. In fact, let's assume that a raider corporation has already purchased 100,000 shares on the open market and is considering making a hostile offer for control. What can the target corporation do to discourage this unfriendly offer?

Lipton's suggestion was for the board of directors to pass a stock plan that would go into effect only if any shareholder amassed a certain percentage (e.g., 20 percent) of the total stock issued. At that point the poison pill would be activated. The corporation would grant rights to all shareholders—other than the raider—to buy additional shares at a steep discount (maybe only a dollar per share).

Suddenly the raider faces a situation it had not anticipated. Consider the differences. If the target corporation's board had not passed the new plan, the raider could buy an additional 100,000 shares at an undervalued price on the open market before making a tender. At that point it would own 200,000 shares (20 percent) and would need only 300,001 more to control over half the 1,000,000 shares outstanding. It could then make a public offer to shareholders for those 300,001 shares at a price well above market—but with a very early expiration date. Shareholders would likely be eager to sell their shares at a premium.

But the playing field looks completely different with a poison pill plan in place. If the plan allows all shareholders other than the raider to buy an additional share for each one they already hold, there will be an additional 800,000 shares in play. Each new share of stock issued reduces the value of existing shares. Now the raider's 200,000 shares constitute about 11 percent of the outstanding shares, a long way from control. Moreover, many of the new shares will be in the hands of stockholders who are loyal to incumbent management and who are likely to refuse any hostile offer by the raider. That makes the success of a hostile offer not only much more expensive but also less likely to succeed. If the raider goes ahead with the hostile offer and is unable to secure control of the corporation, its actions will have effectively diluted the value of the stock it still owns. The raider will be left with 200,000 shares out of a total of 1,800,000 instead of the pre–poison pill total of 1,000,000. Each new share of stock issued reduces the value of existing shares.

Lipton correctly predicted that the new environment created by the existence of the poison pill plan would deter raiders from taking actions that might trigger it. If a corporation wanted to acquire another corporation, it made sense to contact the incumbent board and attempt to arrange a "friendly" takeover.

Of course, raider corporations and their lawyers did not surrender meekly. They challenged the legality of the poison pill defense, but courts upheld its legality.[45] Eventually over four hundred corporations passed versions of Lipton's poison pill.

The social consequences of the "poison pill" are still hotly debated. Its critics claim that it permits an ineffective management to insulate itself from shareholders' attempts to get full dollar for their investments. Defenders say it prevents corporate raiders from reaping unseemly profits by manipulating shareholder short term greed at the expense of longer term corporate profits. Perhaps both sides have a part of the truth. But all sides seem to recognize Lipton's genius in creating the defense; he proved himself a worthy heir to Samuel C. T. Dodd and other trickster corporate counselors.

Abe Fortas

While Dodd and Lipton were counsels to corporations, government lawyers can also play the trickster role. In fact, my personal favorite trickster counselor tale involves a government lawyer, Abe

Fortas.[46] Later in his career, Fortas was not only the premier corporate lawyer in Washington, DC, but he also served as a justice on the US Supreme Court. He started his legal career as one of the young lawyers who worked for federal New Deal agencies in the 1930s.

While still in his twenties, Fortas was appointed general counsel to the Public Works Administration (PWA), one of the New Deal's most successful agencies. About this time, Fortas became a friend of a newly elected congressman from West Texas named Lyndon Johnson, who had a strong interest in constructing the Marshall Ford Dam over the lower Colorado River. Johnson supported the dam not only because it would provide needed electrical power to West Texas, but also because the general contractor for the project was Herman Root, a political power in Texas, who would become Johnson's major financial contributor.

Root had a problem that Johnson hoped Fortas could solve. To make a very long (and very interesting[47]) story short, Root had built the 268-foot high Marshall Ford Dam at a cost of $27 million. But there was funding only for 235 feet (or $24.5 million) of the project. This left Root $2.5 million short. He had worked the numbers and determined that 190 feet of the dam could be justified as a proper expenditure under federal programs for generating electrical power. Another 45 feet could be funded by the Bureau of Reclamation as a project to prevent flooding. But no one could come up with a legal theory that justified funds for the remaining 33 feet—which would supply the $2.5 million that constituted Root's profit on the project.

Johnson brought the problem to his friend Fortas in hope that funding might be provided by Fortas's agency, the PWA. At first glance there seemed to be an insurmountable objection to PWA funding. The PWA was not authorized to engage in either power generation projects or flood control projects. To a lesser lawyer, the discussion would have ended there, but Fortas was a legal genius. The textual prohibition on PWA funding of power and flood control projects just afforded him an opportunity to demonstrate that genius.

Fortas conceded that the PWA could not fund a flood control project or a power generating project, but he decided that the dam Root had built was neither a power generation project nor a flood control project. It was a different legal entity altogether: a hybrid public works project that provided *both* power generation and flood control. The argument is not quite as bizarre as it first sounds. By providing both power and preventing floods, the project would provide two public benefits for the price of one.

Fortas persuaded his superiors to accept his ingenious reasoning. The citizens of West Texas got their dam, and Herman Root got his money. I've seen the Marshall Ford Dam; to the naked eye it seems to be a construction of steel and concrete. But Fortas's legal vision was able to transform it into a legal layer cake comprised of a 33-foot public works project sandwiched between a 190-foot power generating dam and a 45-foot flood control project.

4. Trickster Judges

Judges might seem less likely to display trickster traits than litigators or counselors. Lawyers are partisans attempting to sell one side of a dispute, while we expect judges to impartially dispense justice from a perspective above the fray. But, perhaps because of legal academia's obsession with the judicial opinion, the case for the trickster judge is quite easy to document.

John Marshall

Legal realists taught us long ago that the structure of a judicial opinion gives its author a good deal of opportunity for both creativity and cunning.[48] Facts have to be characterized and legal texts have to be interpreted, and characterization and interpretation are never neutral acts; they tilt toward one resolution or another.[49] But the oracular style of the judicial opinion does not require, or even permit, the judge to admit to the existence of these opportunities for creativity. It almost demands a gap between the judge's thought processes and the form of his or her written opinion.[50]

The truth is that, in difficult cases, there is no precut, legally correct decision for the judge to "discover," only a mass of legal materials from which to construct the "law of the case." The opinion is not expected to be a diary of the judge's ruminations; it's a highly crafted argument geared to persuade the reader that the decision reached was required by law. In this enterprise, judges employ various rhetorical devices to highlight certain materials and minimize the relevance of others. Since there is now a substantial literature documenting how judges use rhetorical devices in constructing their opinions,[51] I will discuss only two judicial opinions, both from my own field of constitutional law, which illustrate both judicial creativity and craft.

The first is Chief Justice John Marshall's opinion in the landmark case of *Marbury v. Madison*.[52] John Marshall is properly remembered as our greatest Chief Justice, but we should remember that before he attained this iconic status he was a politician, and before that a very accomplished appellate advocate in the courts of Virginia.[53] Thomas Jefferson opposed Marshall in politics and disliked him as a person, but he made a comment that testifies to his grudging admiration for Marshall the lawyer: "So great is his sophistry you must never give him an affirmative answer or you will be forced to grant his conclusion. Why, if he were to ask me if it were daylight or not, I'd reply, 'Sir, I don't know. I can't tell.'"[54]

The *Marbury* case afforded Marshall the opportunity to exhibit the full range of his legal genius. It involved a lawsuit that was rife with political implications. The events that precipitated it took place in 1801, in the last few hours of the presidency of John Adams. The Federalist Adams had lost his bid for reelection to the Republican Thomas Jefferson, and partisan ill will dominated the interactions between the parties. In the waning days of his term, Adams filled some newly authorized justice of the peace positions with stalwart Federalist appointees. The appointments were made and confirmed, and signed by Adams's Secretary of State, the very same John Marshall who would later hear the case. All the commissions but one were delivered to the appointees. The plaintiff Marbury was the one appointee who did not receive his commission. When the oversight was discovered, Jefferson's Secretary of

State, James Madison, took the position that the undelivered appointment was a legal nullity and refused to recognize it. Marbury promptly filed a petition for an original writ in the Supreme Court, asking the court to order Madison to obey the law and deliver his judicial commission immediately.

The case became a political sensation. Adams had appointed Marshall as chief justice before leaving office, and Federalist partisans expected the Federalist-controlled court to stand up to what they saw as Madison's defiance of law in refusing Marbury his judgeship. But Marshall knew that issuing the writ would endanger the court's very existence. If the court were to grant Marbury's writ, the Jefferson administration would at best blithely ignore it. That would show the fledgling Supreme Court to be impotent in the face of political opposition. Still worse, the Democratic congress might impeach the judges who handed down such an opinion. Marshall found himself in a trap. If he ruled against Marbury, he would be conceding power to the hated Republican administration. If he ruled for him, the court would either be ignored or attacked.

Marshall appeared to be in a no-win situation.[55] But he saw the situation as an opportunity to win what many believe to be the greatest of all Supreme Court victories. He escaped the trap by ruling against Marbury's claim for relief, but he did so by a doctrinal route that established the Federalist-controlled Supreme Court's authority to invalidate legislation passed by the Republican-controlled Congress. He conceded on the small issue of Marbury's appointment in order to win on the larger issue of the Supreme Court's supremacy in interpreting the Constitution.

Let's look at how he accomplished this neat trick. Early in his opinion, Marshall appears very sympathetic to Marbury's claim. He rules that the appointment did in fact vest when signed, and therefore it did not have to be delivered for Marbury to have a legal right to his judgeship. He also agrees that Marbury has called for the proper remedy in mandamus. There is no doubt that a congressional law gives the Supreme Court the authority to hear such cases as a matter of original jurisdiction. But then Marshall finds a flaw in Marbury's claim; it assumed that Congress had the power to grant the Supreme Court original jurisdiction in cases like this. Perhaps the congressional law granting the authority is itself unconstitutional.

The most famous part of the *Marbury* opinion is where Marshall considers whether the court has the power to invalidate a congressional law it deems in violation of the Constitution.[56] Here Marshall gives us an excellent example of a judge's clever use of rhetoric. Marshall begins by announcing that what seems to be a difficult issue is actually legally quite simple; he cavalierly asserts that the question of the court's power to declare a statute unconstitutional is "deeply interesting...but happily [it is] not of an intricacy proportioned to its interest."[57] This is clearly a disingenuous statement, since the legitimacy of judicial review had always been a very controversial constitutional issue.

Marshall then asserts the uncontroversial proposition that the Constitution articulates the extent of the powers of the various branches of the national government. Once the reader accepts that premise, the logic Jefferson so admired and feared takes charge. If the Constitution is paramount, it must take precedence over ordinary legislation. This is especially true in the case of a written constitution. And since courts by their very nature have the authority and duty to "say what the law is,"[58] if a congressional law is repugnant to the Constitution, it is the court's duty to say so. Marshall then gives a seemingly simple example to illustrate his point. "The constitution declares that 'no bill of attainder or ex post facto law shall be passed.' If, however, such a bill should be passed, and a person should be prosecuted under it, must the court condemn to death those victims whom the constitution deems to preserve?"[59] To the reader, the answer is obvious; the court could not condone an extralegal homicide; it would have the right and duty to declare the congressional law invalid.

At first reading, Marshall's argument seems incontestable, but upon reflection we can see that it appears so only because he has smuggled in a very controversial assumption—the fact that the congressional law at issue is indeed unconstitutional. This might be true in some cases, like Marshall's convenient example of Congress explicitly passing an ex post facto law in spite of the fact that the constitutional text clearly forbids such legislation. Here the reader is forced to accept his conclusion that the court must place the constitutional command above the legislation that contradicts it.

But the constitutionality of a congressional law may sometimes be in dispute, because the constitutional text is often ambiguous. That was in fact the case with the congressional law expanding the court's original jurisdiction to hear Marbury's case. The text of Article III does set out certain types of cases the Supreme Court can hear under its original jurisdiction, but the text does not say whether Congress can grant the court *additional* areas of original jurisdiction. Marshall argued that the text's explicit grant of original jurisdiction in certain areas precludes Congress from adding other areas, but that's an argument, not a necessary logical conclusion. Reasonable people (like members of Congress) might believe that the text permitted Congress to add additional areas of original jurisdiction. And if this were the case, there might be good reason for the court to defer to the judgment of its coequal branch. In other words, Marshall's opinion makes the legitimacy of judicial review appear an easy question, but in fact it is not. And Marshall's example of the ex post facto law is a striking bit of rhetoric, but in a sense it is beside the point.[60]

But we must remember that the fact that the issue is more difficult than Marshall admits does not make his decision wrong. He is only doing what all talented lawyers do: putting his best case forward using rhetorical strategies to persuade the reader that his controversial conclusion is, in fact, required by law.

There is a second level of cunning in the opinion that is even more ingenious. In dismissing Marbury's claim, Marshall has avoided the peril of directly confronting the Republican Congress; but he has done more than play good defense. He advanced his own legal and political agenda. His Republican adversaries got the result they wanted in the refusal of Marbury's claim for relief, but this result was inextricably tied to the ruling that the court had authority to review the constitutionality of congressional legislation. Marshall had now established the authority of the federalist-controlled court to declare legislation passed by the Republican Congress unconstitutional. You might say that Marshall had stooped to conquer. This newly discovered power of judicial review is the basis of the Supreme Court's power and prestige today.[61]

There's yet a third level of Marshall's cunning. Usually judges consider the court's authority to hear a case first and only consider the substantive merits if there is jurisdiction. Therefore, in the natural course of events, we would expect that the court in the *Marbury* case would first discuss the issue of jurisdiction and then, having decided that it does not have jurisdiction, simply dismiss Marbury's suit. But Marshall instead left jurisdiction for last. Marshall reversed the normal practice so he could announce that Marbury had a legal right to his commission and that the court had authority (in cases where it did have jurisdiction) to order the secretary of state to honor it.

The unorthodox structure of his opinion "allowed him to announce the court as guarantor of a nonpartisan rule of law that limited all three branches of government."[62] Marshall's legal conclusion was that the court had no jurisdiction to rule on the merits, but he still discussed them at length. The Federalists accepted his discussion of the substantive merits because they were focused on the small issue of whether Marbury would be a justice of the peace. Marshall saw that there were much larger issues at hand.

Antonin Scalia

Marbury v. Madison was decided a long time ago, when there were few prior decisions to guide judges in making decisions. One might think that the interpretive freedom John Marshall demonstrated in that case was only a product of a porous legal system with few prior cases to rein in judicial creativity. But, I think Justice Antonin Scalia's majority opinion in the 1990 case of *Employment Division v. Smith*[63] will disabuse the reader of the idea that prior precedents effectively curb judicial creativity.

Before studying Scalia's performance in the *Smith* case, let's take a whirlwind ride through the history of American constitutional law from John Marshall's time to the present. The most important constitutional event was the passage in 1868 of the Fourteenth Amendment, with its guarantees of due process and equal protection of the laws. At first the Supreme Court gave limited, narrow interpretations of the due process and equal protection clauses, but in the twentieth century the court increasingly saw the two clauses as important restrictions on state power. We have already discussed the landmark case of *Brown v. Board of Education*, in which the Warren Court (with Thurgood Marshall's help) ruled that the equal protection clause invalidated state systems of racially segregated schools. In other cases the Warren Court also interpreted the term "liberty" in the due process clause to incorporate many of the protections of the Bill of Rights, thereby making them applicable to state laws.

A good example of the Warren Court expanding the applicability of the Bill of Rights through the due process clause is the case of *Sherbert v. Verner*.[64] Sherbert, a member of the Seventh Day Adventist Church, was denied unemployment benefits by the state of South Carolina because she refused to accept jobs that required her to work on Saturday, her religion's Sabbath. The state argued that she had not complied with the state law's requirement that she accept any "suitable position when offered," even if the job required working Saturdays. She in turn contended that the state's conditioning her benefits on the acceptance of a job that violated her religious obligations constituted a violation of her First Amendment right to the free exercise of religion, as incorporated in the Fourteenth Amendment's due process clause.

In an opinion by Justice William Brennan, the Supreme Court agreed with Ms. Sherbert. The court not only ruled that South Carolina's law violated Ms. Sherbert's free exercise rights, it also set in place a new constitutional rule that would be applied in future cases. Now, when a state took action that impacted an individual's free exercise rights, it would be ruled unconstitutional unless the state could show that the regulation contributed to accomplishment of a "compelling state interest" and that it was the "least restrictive means" of achieving that interest. In ordinary English, this meant that the state had to show not only that the regulation helped achieve an important state goal, but also that the regulation was the only effective way of achieving it.

In Sherbert's case, South Carolina had claimed that the compelling need to prevent fraudulent claims justified its use of the requirement to accept any work offered. The State reasoned that if anyone could claim a religious objection to working on Saturdays, the state's employment insurance funds would soon be depleted. Justice Brennan did not contest the state's compelling interest in preventing fraudulent claims; instead he held that the State had not shown that its total ban on religiously based refusals was the least restrictive means of achieving that goal. He felt that the state had just assumed that allowing claimants to refuse jobs that violated their religious duties would lead to widespread fraud; it had not looked into the possibility of alternative effective ways to combat fraud that would have been less burdensome on religious scruples. The Warren Court had struck again, this time vastly expanding the rights of individuals to follow the dictates of their religions.

The *Sherbert v. Verner* rule was followed in numerous Supreme Court cases in the twenty-seven years leading up to the *Smith* case.[65] In practical terms, the *Sherbert* case meant that members of smaller religions were now exempt from state laws that required them to violate their religious beliefs. Civil libertarians applauded the court's protection of the rights of members of small religions to follow the tenets of their faith; people like Ms. Sherbert now had the same freedom to practice their religion as members of larger religions whose religiously motivated conduct was seldom interfered with by state law.

But not everyone agreed. Many conservatives thought *Sherbert* was a prime example of the Warren Court's "judicial activism," a term they used to describe what they saw as the court's tendency to ignore the policy choices of democratically elected legislators in favor of its own views on social issues. Unless clearly required by the constitutional text, constitutional conservatives felt such activism was inappropriate for nonelected judges. Often liberals seemed to assume that critics of the court just disagreed with the results the Warren Court reached. But conservatives claimed they were not just objecting to the result the court reached in a case like *Sherbert*, but also to its method in reaching it. Conservatives were not hostile to people practicing their religion; they just didn't think it was the business of nonelected judges to second-guess the policy decisions of state legislators without a clear constitutional mandate.

In its purest form, the conservative critique of the Warren Court was that the Supreme Court had no right to inject concerns about free exercise of religion into cases involving state laws because the free exercise clause was part of the First Amendment, which applied only to acts of Congress. Even those who would allow some consideration of free exercise principles in reviewing state legislation believed that the review should be restrained and limited to situations where the law explicitly discriminated against religious objections to state laws. It certainly should not apply to a state law that applied equally to everyone. Courts were not meant to second-guess decisions state legislators were elected to make. The *Sherbert* rule's amorphous "compelling state interest/least restrictive means" test constituted exactly this type of judicial meddling, judicial misbehavior that threatened the future of constitutional government in America.

Antonin Scalia was the only child of an immigrant father who had earned a doctorate in literature and went on to teach at Brooklyn College. Scalia was a standout student at Jesuit-run Xavier High School in New York City, where he was known for his acting skills (starring in *Macbeth* in his senior year) and for his religious devotion.[66] Scalia attended Georgetown University (also a Jesuit institution) in Washington, DC, where he was the class valedictorian. From Georgetown, Scalia continued on to Harvard Law

School, where he was chosen for the law review and the prestigious position of Note Editor. After graduation, he worked a short time for a corporate firm before accepting a teaching post at the University of Chicago Law School.

He made no attempt to conceal his conservative legal views; at Chicago he was involved in the early days of the Federalist Society, a conservative organization founded to combat the Warren Court's "activism." From Chicago he went to a position on a federal court of appeals, where he served until he was appointed to the Supreme Court in 1986 by President Ronald Reagan, who was looking for conservative justices to roll back the legacy of the Warren Court.

Scalia quickly began to be noticed. From the beginning, he was willing to engage in the colloquies between justices and counsel that enliven Supreme Court oral arguments, and this type of interaction provided an excellent showcase for his quick wit. He was not only willing to advance what were then considered extremely conservative views, but he was able to illustrate them with rhetorical flourishes that made dry legal analyses come to life. At first Scalia's rhetorical skills were mostly relegated to concurrences and dissents, but as the court as a whole grew more conservative, he began to be assigned authorship of majority opinions.

One such opinion was in the case of *Employment Division v. Smith*.[67] The case concerned two members of the Native American Church who were fired from their jobs as counselors at a drug rehabilitation project because they had ingested peyote during a church service, a violation of Oregon's drug laws. They said they only used peyote as part of the ceremonies at the Native American Church. They applied for unemployment benefits but were denied because the state claimed their violation of a criminal statute constituted "misconduct" that disqualified them from unemployment benefits. The workers argued that their use of peyote in a religious service was protected by the free exercise clause and could not be used to deny them benefits. The primary case they submitted in support of their position was *Sherbert v. Verner*.

Briefs were filed and the case was argued orally before the court. During the conference where the judges vote on which side should win, six justices stated that they intended to uphold Oregon's decision to deny unemployment benefits. Chief Justice William Rehnquist assigned Scalia the job of drafting the opinion. Here Scalia had a choice to make. He could write a narrow opinion based on *Sherbert*'s compelling state interest test, finding that Oregon's law passed the test; this would receive the support of six justices. Or he could go after bigger game, challenging the Warren Court's *Sherbert* rule head on. If he went this route, he would lose the vote of Justice Sandra Day O'Connor but still have a five-vote majority.

Scalia decided to attack the *Sherbert v. Verner* test itself. Choosing this route was quite daring, because over of a period of almost thirty years the Supreme Court had several times endorsed the *Sherbert* test as the appropriate rule in free exercise cases.[68] Now Scalia faced another difficult choice. Should he explicitly overrule *Sherbert v. Verner*? He could simply say that *Sherbert* and all the cases that followed it had been wrongly decided and overrule them. But the Supreme Court is reluctant to admit that past decisions, especially relatively recent decisions, were mistakenly decided, for the good reason that the public will stop trusting a court that frequently changes its mind.

So Scalia decided not to explicitly overrule *Sherbert v. Verner*. He would therefore have to "distinguish" it by showing that *Sherbert* and the cases that followed it involved facts so dissimilar to the present case that he was not bound by them. But that would seem to be an almost impossible task, since the factual situations in *Sherbert* and the other prior precedents often seemed quite similar to those in the *Smith* case. *Sherbert* itself, like *Smith*, involved the refusal to grant unemployment benefits to an applicant who said the applicable state rule violated her free exercise rights. But Scalia was undeterred.

It turns out that Justice Scalia has set out, in his customary vivid prose style, his views on how a judge should approach prior precedents.

> Within...a precedent-bound common-law system, it is critical for the lawyer, or the judge, to establish whether the case at hand falls within a principle that has already been decided. Here the technique—or the art, or the game—of "distinguishing" earlier cases. It is an art or a game, rather than a science, because what constitutes the "holding" of an earlier case is not well-defined, and can be adjusted to suit the occasion...The American law student's image of the great judge—the Holmes, the Cardozo—is the man (or woman) who has the intelligence to discern the best rule of law for the case at hand, and then the skill to perform the broken-field running through earlier cases that leaves him free to impose that rule: distinguishing one prior case on the left, straight-arming another on the right, high-stepping away from another precedent about to tackle him from the rear, until (bravo!) he reaches the goal—good law.[69]

Now I want to make it very clear that Justice Scalia is only talking here about judges operating within a purely common-law system, with no input from statutes or the Constitution, where he thinks respect for democracy should restrain the judge's creativity. He says he is not talking about writing Supreme Court opinions on constitutional issues. Still, I think Justice Scalia's description of a common law judge's "broken-field running" through hostile precedents has a good deal of value in describing Scalia's own handling of prior precedents in the *Smith* opinion. I will leave it to the reader to judge whether I am correct.

At the beginning of his opinion, Justice Scalia makes what at first glance seems to be simply an incredible statement.

> We have never held that an individual's religious beliefs excuse him from compliance with an otherwise valid law prohibiting conduct that the State is free to regulate.[70]

This is a rejection of the holding and constitutional rule adopted in *Sherbert v. Verner*. Did not the Supreme Court in that case say that the free exercise clause excused Ms. Sherbert from obeying valid South Carolina law on accepting job offers? But before we dismiss Scalia's statement, let's watch the trickster judge (or "broken-field runner") go to work on those prior precedents that appear to undercut his bold statement.

One of the cases that appeared to endorse the *Sherbert* rule was *United States v. Lee*.[71] Lee was a member of the Old Amish faith, which condemned the paying of taxes to civil governments. Lee claimed that requiring him to pay social security taxes was a violation of his free exercise rights under the reasoning of *Sherbert v. Verner*. The Supreme Court agreed that the *Sherbert* rule should be applied, but held that the social security tax scheme passed the compelling state interest test. Scalia jumped on this discrepancy between the *Lee* majority's endorsement of the *Sherbert* rule and how they actually applied the rule. The court actually held that the imposition of nondiscriminatory burden on religiously motivated conduct did not violate the free exercise clause. So from this perspective, it supported his proposition that the court had never allowed a claim of free exercise to excuse an individual from obeying a valid state law. Scalia argued that *Lee*, properly viewed, did not support the claims of the peyote smokers in Smith; it supported the state.

But there also were Supreme Court opinions that not only applied the *Sherbert* test, but also held that a state law had violated it. Most prominent was the case of *Wisconsin v. Yoder*.[72] *Yoder* involved members of the Amish Mennonite faith claiming that Wisconsin's compulsory school attendance laws violated the tenets of their religion in requiring their children to attend school after eighth grade. Even though the fine they were required to pay for violating the compulsory attendance law was quite small, the Supreme Court applied the *Sherbert* test and found that the compulsory attendance law violated the parents' free exercise rights.

Here was a free exercise of religion case that opposed Scalia not only in applying the *Sherbert* rule, but also in finding the state action unconstitutional. And the factual situations in *Yoder* and *Smith* seemed similar. In *Yoder* the state law required school attendance, while in *Smith* it forbade using drugs, but both were neutral laws that burdened free exercise rights. It appeared that *Yoder* should control the decision in *Smith*.

But here Scalia engaged in some of the "broken-field running" he so admired in common law judges. He saw the two cases as different legal animals altogether. *Yoder* was a "hybrid" case that involved two types of constitutional rights—the right of free exercise of religion and the privacy right of parents to raise their children as they deemed fit. *Smith* only involved free exercise rights. By construing *Yoder* as a different category of case, he escaped its precedential force. And once he disposed of *Yoder*, Scalia could still contend that the Supreme Court had never held that religiously motivated conduct was exempt from a generally applicable legislative prohibition neutrally applied.

Scalia then continued to undercut the precedential pull of *Sherbert* by calling attention to another line of cases where the court had not applied it to free exercise claims. One such case was *Goldman v. Weinberger*,[73] in which an air force officer who was an orthodox Jew challenged a dress code that forbade him from wearing a yarmulke while on duty. The Supreme Court upheld the dress code without applying the *Sherbert* rule. Since the Supreme Court has always treated military rules with great deference, the *Goldman* case had commonly been seen as an example of the "military" exception to the *Sherbert* rule, with no relevance to Smith's claim.

But Scalia had a different slant on *Goldman*; he saw that once one stopped focusing on in its military context, *Goldman* was an excellent of example of the rule he was proposing. The free exercise clause did not immunize believers from the requirements of a generally applicable, otherwise valid rule. *Goldman* was now not merely a limited exception to the *Sherbert* rule; it was a precursor to its replacement.

Now all that were left standing were cases involving unemployment benefits. Since the *Smith* case was an unemployment benefits case, these cases would seem to be of special relevance to its resolution. One such case was *Thomas v. Review Bd. of Indiana Employment Div., Department of Human Resources*.[74] Thomas was a Jehovah's Witness who left his job when his employer decided to focus on the production of munitions. Since this violated Thomas's pacifist religious belief, he left his job and applied for unemployment payments. The state refused to grant them because it did not believe religious reasons constituted "good cause" for refusing work under the unemployment scheme. In *Thomas*, the Supreme Court ruled 8–1 that Thomas's free exercise rights had been violated. This was not a surprising result, since the facts so closely resembled those in *Sherbert v. Verner*.

Scalia did not overrule *Thomas* or *Sherbert*. Instead he "distinguished" them by limiting them to their facts, the individualized application of open-ended "good cause" conditions on the receipt of unemployment benefits. *Sherbert* was not formally overruled but was made innocuous. It was no longer the master rule for free exercise jurisprudence; it was only a footnote relevant in the small number of unemployment cases that involved "good cause" restrictions. It certainly had no precedential value in the *Smith* context, where religiously motivated conduct violated an explicit statutory prohibition. Touchdown!

All the contrary precedent having been artfully discarded, Scalia was able to announce a replacement for the *Sherbert v. Verner* rule: "If prohibiting the free exercise of religion is merely the incidental effect of a generally applicable and otherwise valid provision, the First Amendment is not violated."[75] Free exercise protections would now only apply to laws that discriminated against religious believers or that involved individualized determinations in the unemployment benefit area.

I think most commentators would agree with Justice Blackmun's comment in his dissent that the *Smith* majority opinion effectuated "a wholesale overturning of settled law concerning the Religion Clauses of our Constitution."[76] But that leaves open the question of whether the *Smith* opinion is "good" law. Of course, the term "good" is ambiguous. Let's consider two senses of "good" that might apply to the *Smith* opinion. "Good" can have a normative cast in the sense of whether the opinion is the best possible interpretation of the constitutional text.

Many commentators, some with excellent conservative credentials, have criticized *Smith* on this normative metric arguing that the opinion does not give sufficient protection to members of small religions who cannot persuade legislatures to protect their religious beliefs. I agree that *Smith* is not a "good" opinion in this sense, yet I recognize that other commentators would disagree with that conclusion.

But here I am more interested in a second sense of "good." Was the decision reached by proper forms of legal argument? I would say it clearly was. Justice Scalia confronted all the relevant precedents and, with one exception,[77] made strong arguments why they did not apply to the case at hand. From a craft perspective, I think that it's more than a "good" opinion; it's a brilliant one.

Judicial creativity, savvy, and guile are necessary ingredients in the recipe that makes our constitutional system work. We have an old constitution that uses abstract terms open to many interpretations.[78] Moreover, it is a very difficult constitution to amend; for better or worse we are therefore stuck with the original text. That text is able to provide answers to new problems only because the Supreme Court since *Marbury v. Madison* has given fresh meanings to the old text. Supreme Court justices like Marshall and Scalia have performed the function that Lewis Hyde ascribes to the trickster—they have provided flexibility so that the constitutional structure is able to adjust to new conditions.

This constitutional dynamic will not end with the *Smith* case. For a time, a reading of the free exercise clause like that found in *Sherbert v. Verner* was the "official" reading and controlled future cases. But slowly another interpretation rose to challenge it. That new interpretation prevailed in *Smith* and now controls, but if history is any predictor of the future, a new challenger will eventually arise to contest *Smith*.

This contrapuntal process is accomplished by judges who themselves are not elected, but who are appointed by elected presidents and confirmed by elected senators. That does not mean that a judge is just a politician who does not run for election. A judge's power is circumscribed by the standards of legal argument. While these standards allow for a great deal of creativity, especially at the Supreme Court level, they are not endlessly elastic. As we will see in the next chapter, sometimes judges go too far.

A legislator just has to vote; he has no constitutional duty to justify the vote one way or another. But a judge must justify his or her decision by the accepted standards of legal argument, considering all the relevant legal data and reconciling them in his or her decision. Sometimes this takes more than logic; it also takes art. A judge must distill a new meaning from the old legal materials and, by so doing, move the system forward while simultaneously it looks back.

John Denvir

5. Too Clever by Half

All the trickster lawyer stories I have told to this point have ended in success. But Lewis Hyde reminds us that in folklore sometimes the Trickster can be too clever for his own good.[79] The same is true for the trickster lawyer. In this chapter, I would like to portray some dangers the trickster identity warns us against. Sometimes trickster lawyers go too far. Here we see two of my trickster lawyer "heroes" in a darker light.

The first is Eliot Spitzer. No one could contest the fact that Spitzer made Wall Street take notice of its duty to protect the small investor. While some questioned the tactics he employed, no one doubted his brilliance, audacity, and savvy. He certainly got the job done, but perhaps sometimes at a high cost, in terms of unfairness to the accused and a coarsening of the legal system.

As I pointed out earlier, there was nothing subtle in Spitzer's approach to prosecution. If he detected a hint of impropriety, he would first issue subpoenas that he hoped would yield evidence of illegal conduct, and then confront the alleged malefactors. They could agree to a settlement in which they would admit culpability and pay a heavy fine, or Spitzer would turn up the heat by filing a civil suit under the Martin Act and call a press conference at which he would lambast the accused firms for outrageous breaches of the public trust. Lurking in the background was the possibility that he might also file a criminal suit against the offending company or its management. Even if the companies could be successful in their legal defenses, for many, the price of vindication was too high to risk. It appears some corporate defendants decided it made more economic sense to cave in to Spitzer's demands than stand on their rights.

I don't feel I have the expertise to judge whether or not Spitzer went too far, but I think it is important to recognize that at some point aggressive prosecution can cross the line into abuse of power. Some critics claimed that Spitzer's "trials by press conference" crossed that line. They were especially critical of his veiled threats of criminal prosecution. A criminal fraud case is easy to file but difficult to prove. However, defendants rightly believed they could not wait for their day in court because the negative publicity from the criminal suit's filing would destroy the market value of their companies.

There is also the issue of professional civility. Eliot Spitzer played hardball all the time. He pushed everything to the limit, whether he was dealing with potential defendants or potential allies like the SEC. The legal profession needs professional civility to perform its important social function of resolving conflicts between antagonists without stoking the fires of hostility. When does an extremely aggressive stance in every individual case begin to erode this level of civility? Spitzer reportedly once referred to himself as a human "steamroller." I don't think this is the best approach for a public official charged with fairly enforcing the laws.

Ironically, Eliot Spitzer's fall was just as precipitous as his rise. He was involved in a sex scandal about halfway through his term as governor and resigned his office. To date, his attempts at a political comeback have been unsuccessful.

The second trickster lawyer I think went too far is Justice Antonin Scalia. There's no doubt that Justice Scalia had a great day as a judge in the *Smith* case. He was no longer writing clever dissents; he was crafting majority opinions that were reshaping the constitutional structure of the nation. One can forgive Scalia if he started to see himself as a master of the legal universe. But sometimes the trickster's cockiness can lead him to take steps he later regrets. Remember, Brer Rabbit would never have had to outsmart Brer Fox if he had not tangled with the Tar-Baby. I think Justice Scalia may someday regret his role in *Bush v. Gore*.[80]

Bush v. Gore is one of the most important and controversial decisions in Supreme Court history; important because is it the only case in which the Supreme Court decided the outcome of a close presidential election, and controversial because most commentators believe the five-justice majority failed to justify its decision by appropriate legal standards.

The presidential race of 2000 was very close, and it turned out that the candidate who was awarded Florida's electoral votes would become president. George W. Bush had a very narrow lead in the first count in that state, but Al Gore's campaign argued that a significant number of Gore votes had been improperly disallowed—a number sufficient to make him the victor. When the Florida Supreme Court ordered a recount of the contested ballots, the Bush campaign asked the US Supreme Court to intervene.

The court accepted the case, and a five-justice majority eventually ruled that the recounts themselves violated the equal protection clause of the Fourteenth Amendment because the Florida Supreme Court had not mandated "specific standards" that would be applied statewide in determining how questionable ballots were to be counted. Having determined a constitutional violation, the majority considered what remedy to impose. Instead of allowing the recounts to continue under uniform standards, it ruled that such a recount could not be completed within the period suggested by federal law. Accordingly, it declared that the recount should not go forward, thereby awarding the Florida electoral votes, and the presidency, to Bush.

Justice Scalia was one of the five justices who signed the majority opinion. The case must have placed Justice Scalia in a very uncomfortable position.

We have every reason to believe that he voted for Republican George W. Bush, for the excellent reason that he agreed with him on the issues. But Justice Scalia had always been a very eloquent critic of "judicial activism," and for a court to determine the winner of a very close election would appear to be the epitome of judicial activism. We have also seen in the *Smith* case that he was an eloquent critic of Supreme Court justices who second-guess the decisions of state officials. And while *Smith* was a due process/free exercise case and *Bush v. Gore* was decided under an equal protection/voting rights theory, Scalia had also been vehemently opposed to using the equal protection clause to overrule state decisions in the voting area.

So there was a split between what Scalia saw as a "good" decision as a matter of result and the decision his prior decisions called for. In fact, the principles that Scalia and his conservative allies espoused in the *Bush v. Gore* opinion would have extended federal judicial involvement in state elections well beyond what the Warren Court had required.

But Scalia and his colleagues wanted to have it both ways. They wanted to award the election to Bush, but without involving the federal courts in other state election issues. So they added a unique proviso to their majority opinion: "Our consideration is limited to the present circumstances, for the problem of equal protection in election cases presents many complexities."[81] This means that the principles used to award the presidency to Bush should never be applied to any other case. After *Bush v. Gore* performed its role of awarding the presidency to the candidate the justices favored, it would become a constitutional orphan with no effect on future cases.

But this contradicts the cardinal rule of constitutional jurisprudence: a principle, once adopted, must be applied across the board to similar cases. In order to prevent judges from picking and choosing winners on a partisan basis, we require them to apply the principles used in the present case to future similar cases. In fact, I can cite no less an authority than Justice Scalia himself for that proposition.

> The Supreme Court of the United States does not sit to announce "unique" dispositions. Its principal function is to establish precedent—that is, to set forth principles of law that every court in America must follow.[82]

Bush v. Gore is the classic example of a "unique" disposition.

In the *Smith* case, Scalia confronted all the appropriate legal materials and by means of craft made them speak the result he desired. In *Bush v. Gore*, he couldn't reconcile the result he desired with the relevant law, so he ruled outside the regime of constitutional discourse. A legislator can make decisions that way, but a judge cannot. He must fit the decision within a reading of past cases and possible future cases. As Margaret Jane Radin succinctly puts it, *"Bush v. Gore* looks like a legal opinion, but it isn't a legal decision, because it is outside the boundaries of acceptable argument."[83]

The majority opinion in *Bush v. Gore* is a partisan document. Of course, many Americans think that all Supreme Court opinions are "political," and I think in one sense they are correct in that be- lief. Judges are not robots; they are human beings with political views that inevitably influence how they read the relevant legal texts. But *Bush v. Gore* is political in a different sense; it is a parti- san political act masquerading as law. Our constitutional system allows a lot of leeway for judicial creativity, especially at the Su- preme Court level. But sometimes the justices go too far and ignore basic premises of legal argument. *Bush v. Gore* is such a case.

I said earlier that I thought Justice Scalia might someday regret his involvement in *Bush v. Gore*. To date he has shown no such remorse. Justice Scalia has been reluctant to defend the opinion on its merits; instead, he has had blunt advice for critics of *Bush v. Gore*: "Get over it!"[84] I hope we don't "get over" *Bush v. Gore*, because if we do it means we have given up on the ideal of a gov- ernment of laws, not of men.

6. Is Guile Good?

My argument has been that the qualities that make lawyers special are not limited to technical skills like knowledge of rules and legal analysis, but also include imagination, savvy, and cunning or guile. I do not claim that all lawyers are tricksters all the time. Sometimes the legal landscape does not allow them enough maneuvering room to employ trickster skills. Other times lawyers are only asked to give clients a neutral picture of the legal pitfalls that confront them. And some lawyers are never tricksters because they do not possess the necessary creativity, savvy, and cunning.

I do not want to suggest that more orthodox skills, like knowledge of legal doctrine and mastery of legal analysis, are not necessary parts of the practice of law. But I do not think these skills constitute the essence of "thinking like a lawyer." I see them as resources the trickster lawyer employs in the larger enterprise of persuasion. So while all lawyers are not tricksters all the time, I believe the best are tricksters at least some of the time. I also believe it is the trickster aspect of the lawyer identity that makes the public both admire and fear us.

I see the trickster as a positive image for lawyers. Still, I recognize that many lawyers will resist the trickster identity because it does not seem to them sufficiently dignified for a learned profession. Here I assume the problem is not with the trickster lawyer's creativity, but rather with the trickster's cunning or guile, two terms I use interchangeably. My goal, therefore, is to show that guile properly understood is a talent lawyers should take pride in, because it permits us to play our important societal role. It is no more than a form of intelligence that can be used for good or bad purposes. Within the adversary system, lawyers mostly use it for good purposes.

What is cunning or guile? Dictionaries tell us that cunning is "skill in devising or using indirect or subtle methods." This seems an accurate description of what I claim the trickster lawyer does. "Cunning" is also defined as the "ability to mislead, trap, or escape an enemy or opponent." One of its synonyms is "deceit." "Guile" is defined as "crafty or deceitful cunning." "Duplicity" and "deceit" are listed as synonyms for it.

Terms like "deceit" and "duplicity" set off alarms of ethical impropriety that give lawyers pause. But I don't believe these pejorative terms should apply to the lawyer's use of cunning or guile. "Deceit" involves making someone believe propositions the deceiver knows to be false. This sense of deceit does not apply to lawyerly guile, because it divides the world of discourse into "true" and "false" propositions.

Lawyers operate in a world where the issue is not between known truths and falsehoods, but between competing candidates for truth. For instance, we seldom know for sure the true mental state of a defendant in a murder trial. We only know that the jury must decide to accept either the prosecution's or the defense's position on the issue of "malice." The defense attorney does not attempt to provide the jury with an impartial summary of the available evidence on that issue; he or she does everything possible to direct the jury to evidence that supports the defense's theory, and to question evidence that supports the prosecution's theory. And the jury knows that is the defense lawyer's job.

I think the pejorative term "deceit" mis-describes the lawyer's actions. Lawyer advocacy is better described as "misdirection" than "deceit"; it is an attempt to direct the audience toward the facts that tilt toward the lawyer's preferred resolution of the issue at hand. I prefer the term "misdirection," because it refers to the act of focusing the audience's attention on certain facets of the situation and distracting them from others.

Take the Karen Silkwood case. It was not a matter of making the jury believe something that is false; it was about persuading them to accept one of two rival theories of what is true. This is not underhanded or sneaky, because the jury knows the role of a plaintiff's attorney. And if they don't, the defense attorney is there to remind them.

We should also be suspicious of the negative connotation of the term "duplicity" when applied to lawyers. "Duplicity" points to a divide between someone's public actions and his or her private beliefs. Once again lawyers do certainly exhibit a form of "doubleness" in their professional activities. For instance, a lawyer who thinks that his client is guilty is ethically forbidden from saying so to the jury. This lack of candor is necessary to the lawyer's societal role, and it is an accepted tool in the arenas in which he or she operates.

I think we should avoid the term "duplicitous," with its pejorative tone, when talking about lawyerly guile. Whether lack of candor is an ethical failing or a valuable professional skill depends on the context. A "good" poker player must be able to bluff if he or she hopes for any success in the game. Yet bluffing consists of hiding from opponents your true evaluation of the strength of your hand.

Similarly, there certainly was a divide between "Honest Abe" Lincoln's public actions and his private thoughts when he asked the witness the seemingly innocent question of whether the moon shone the night of the murder. But his disingenuous cordiality was a tactic necessary to perform his role as defense attorney. Just as I suggest that lawyerly guile is better described as "misdirection" rather than deceit, I think that in the adversary context we should substitute the more neutral term "disingenuousness" for "duplicity," because it keeps the descriptive core without the undeserved pejorative connotation. "Disingenuous" is an antonym of "naïve," and no lawyer claims to be naïve.

Litigators are not the only lawyers who are guilty of "misdirection" and "disingenuousness." In freeing his client Standard Oil from the control of state regulators, Samuel C. T. Dodd made sure to pay close attention to the letter of the laws as he quietly evaded their spirit.

The same can be said of judges. I think Justice Scalia's opinion in the *Smith* case is an excellent example; Scalia found himself in a situation where the applicable "rule" seemed to favor one result, but the recent case holdings were in tension with the rule. Since the holdings were more favorable to the resolution he preferred, his response was to ignore the rule and focus on the holdings of the cases and an alternative rule they might support. This is an example of guile as misdirection. He was also guilty of a certain disingenuousness because his opinion pretends to do no more than decide the case before him, while his true goal was to overturn a major doctrinal legacy of the Warren Court. Here both misdirection and disingenuousness are accepted parts of legal argument.

Even if we conclude there is nothing ethically improper in the lawyer's use of guile within the context of the system, there still is the question of whether guile improves the system. I think it does because guile permits lawyers to act as catalysts, giving them the rhetorical space to propose new ways to look at the problem at hand. It is true that lawyers are only attempting to advance their clients' interests, but in so doing they expand the range of alternatives from which the larger legal and political systems can choose in creating society's future. There are of course cases where lawyers do not further the social good, but even with these we must remember that the lawyer never has the final say with regard to results. Like Hermes in the Homeric Hymns, the trickster lawyer can propose a new future, but higher authorities like Apollo must approve it if it is to take effect.

Let's review how lawyers work their professional magic. First, remember that lawyers deal with laws that are often ambiguous and capable of more than one interpretation. Second, the facts relevant to a legal problem are often changing and in dispute, making them open to more than one characterization. Third, the Anglo-American legal tradition has adopted an adversary system of justice that invites lawyers to use legal ambiguity and factual indeterminacy to their clients' advantage. Finally, the adversary system puts participants on notice that lawyers will use all avenues arguably within the law to advance their clients' interests. When both sides of a case are represented by skilled counsel using their creativity to generate a winning argument, the result is that the universe of possible outcomes is expanded, which benefits society as a whole. It's the judge or jury that chooses between the solutions offered.

We have already seen several examples of this dynamic. The defendants in *Brown v. Board of Education* believed that the meaning of the equal protection clause could only apply in the contexts that its drafters consciously contemplated. But Thurgood Marshall saw that a broader interpretation of the text's meaning could lead to the end of segregated public schools in America. So he fashioned an argument that led the Supreme Court to accept the NAACP's broader vision of equal protection.

Would it be a better system if the Supreme Court had only heard the school district's view? I think we were fortunate Marshall was allowed to show that the Delphic term "equal protection of the laws" can carry more than one meaning, and that he persuaded the court that his preferred meaning better reflected our constitutional ideals. Marshall didn't make the decision, but his arguments were an essential part of a decision process that yielded a constitutional rule that both conservatives and liberals now accept as legitimate.

Legal counselors like Samuel C. T. Dodd and Martin Lipton also provide society a valuable service. Dodd faced a situation where a corporation with national scope could no longer operate efficiently in a network dominated by local regulatory agencies. He solved the problem by creating a new legal entity, the trust, which freed large corporations from the conflicting and parochial regulations of state governments.

Some say his creation enabled corporations to be the economic engines of our national prosperity. Others see trusts as an end run around the democratic control of private wealth necessary to preserve the public good. No matter which side we believe is correct in this philosophical debate, let's remember that Congress, not Dodd, made the final decision. Congress disallowed the trust vehicle itself, but it created new forms of corporate structure that responded to the problems created by the former system of local control. Dodd's solution was not the one finally chosen, but it was a necessary catalyst in the process that generated a solution that is now generally accepted. Once again, whatever one's view of the role of corporations in American society, it seems clear that Dodd's ingenuity enriched the debate.

We see the same dynamic in Martin Lipton's invention of the poison pill. Corporate raiders like T. Boone Pickens had found a way to game the system by making corporate boards offers they could not refuse. Lipton's genius found a way to make such offers much less attractive to raiders. They cried "foul" and sought relief from the courts, but the courts approved the poison pill as an appropriate tool to protect current shareholders. You do not have to approve of the poison pill as policy to applaud the fact that Lipton expanded the range of possible solutions available.

The trickster work of the judge also produces a public good. As a societal institution, the law must appear stable while at the same time evolving to meet new conditions. The trickster judge's adroit use of rhetorical devices permits the law to perform these seemingly contradictory functions. He or she takes ambiguity and turns it into a resource for change. John Marshall's performance in *Marbury v. Madison* is an example of a trickster judge acting as an agent of change. In effect, Marshall proposed a possible future for American constitutionalism that later Supreme Courts were free to accept or reject. In fact, later Supreme Courts have embraced judicial review, and attempts to amend the constitutional text to forbid it have been unsuccessful.

Our political culture has approved John Marshall's invention. And other democracies around the world have copied our constitutional practice by explicitly creating constitutional courts with the power to declare legislation unconstitutional. Marshall's "trick" is now considered a fundamental aspect of the rule of law.

John Denvir

7. Ethics

I have tried to present an argument for the positive role lawyers play in American society, but I must add an important caveat that raises ethical issues for the profession as a whole and for individual lawyers. My picture of trickster lawyers has them operating within the discipline of a well-functioning adversary system, but the sad truth is that most Americans have no access to such a system because they cannot pay the lordly fees lawyers charge. A dispute in which one party is represented by skilled counsel and the other is unrepresented, or represented by a lawyer unable to bring sufficient time and resources to the case, is ripe for injustice.

It is true that some types of cases, like personal injury litigation, are self-financing because the lawyer's fee is a percentage of the recovery. But lawyers will only engage in such contingent fee contracts when the anticipated recovery is large enough to justify the lawyer's time. Professor Deborah Rhode of Stanford Law School estimates that plaintiffs with valid personal injury claims of less than $150,000 are effectively fenced out of the system because a smaller award is not sufficient to justify a lawyer's time.[85] While some low-income Americans can get representation from publicly funded legal service lawyers, the types of cases these lawyers can handle are limited by law. Even indigent clients who have an eligible case find it very difficult to find a lawyer, because funding for free legal services is so small compared to the need.[86]

Some lawyers will take cases on a pro bono basis, but studies show that the total amount of such free service makes only a small contribution. The average pro bono commitment of an American lawyer amounts to about one half hour per week, and much of that time is spent helping friends, family, or charities that serve the wealthy.[87] The result is many potential plaintiffs with meritorious cases cannot find representation, and many defendants with good defenses cannot find a lawyer to represent them. A study by the NYU Law School Brennan Center for Justice found that 60–90 percent of people whose homes were foreclosed on following the 2008 financial meltdown were not represented by counsel in court.[88]

Obviously, a legal system in which only one side has a lawyer is unlikely to produce just results, and the cleverer the attorney, the less just the result is likely to be. This situation raises a major question for the legal profession about its role in seeing that all Americans have access to legal services. It also raises ethical questions for individual lawyers about their role in handling cases in which their adversary is not represented by counsel. What are the ethical responsibilities for a bank's lawyer who discovers the defendant in a foreclosure proceeding is unrepresented by counsel?

Other questions about the use of lawyerly guile arise even when both sides are represented. These consist of what I would call "lawyer overreaching"—using tactics that go too far. For instance, Eliot Spitzer may well have gone too far in some of his prosecutorial tactics.

It is important to start with the principle that the trickster lawyer must be more than a trickster. He or she is not a professional "outlaw." A lawyer is a professional, licensed by the state and bound by the law. If we find that trickster lawyers are using tactics that give them an unfair advantage there is no reason why the Bar or the legislature cannot outlaw those practices. In fact, many of the twentieth century's civil and criminal procedural reforms prevented one party in a lawsuit from taking unfair advantage.

Lawyers are also bound by ethical principles enforced by professional discipline. In addition, I think lawyers should be encouraged to think through a personal professional code governing how they will use, or refuse to use, their professional skills. That code should focus on concrete ethical problems likely to arise in the individual lawyer's practice. Here I think the trickster identity is a resource because it awakens us to the fact that to do our jobs well, our actions often take us right up to the border between effective advocacy and deceit in the pejorative sense.

My experience is that the most dangerous ethical conflicts lawyers face are the ones they ignore. Ethical dilemmas we recognize can be navigated. Unfortunately, there is too often tacit agreement to ignore certain ethical problems that might interfere with current practices. That's all the more reason why a trickster ethics must be individual and sometimes contrarian.

I also think the individual lawyer's code should go beyond ethics to consider the personal values that help situate the lawyer's professional activities within a matrix that leads to a professionally and personally fulfilling life.

One value concerns what I will call "authenticity." An attractive quality of tricksters like Brer Rabbit is that they are always—win or lose—acting in their own interest. Of course, this cannot be directly true for lawyers who are hired to act for others. But while we have to accept the fact that our personal values and those of our clients cannot always coincide, it might be a rather inauthentic professional life if they never did.

Traditionally lawyers have been taught they have no ethical obligation to represent any given client, except in the case of an "unpopular client" unable to secure representation elsewhere. Most firms are willing to represent any client able to pay their fees. One of the major differences between the technocrat lawyer and the trickster lawyer is how each views the connection between law and politics.

The technocrat pictures law as a politically neutral game in which a lawyer's only concern is to represent the client well. Trickster lawyers are strong proponents of the duty of zealous advocacy, but they also think law has a political impact, and they see the lawyer's role as creative more than technical. Accordingly, they will be more aware of the political consequences of their labors.

We must of course remember that law is more than a vocation; it is also how we earn a living. Only a fool or a saint would be unconcerned about the remunerative aspects of practicing law. Still, I believe lawyers would live more fulfilling lives if, in making employment decisions, they included the need for a supportive workplace where they can do creative work, at least some of which is aimed at making what they feel is a better world.

We are told that Samuel C. T. Dodd did not share his client John D. Rockefeller's enthusiasm for laissez-faire capitalism, but I am sure this political difference did not prevent Dodd from taking a great deal of professional pride in his invention of the Standard Oil Trust. Yet I cannot help but believe that Thurgood Marshall took a more personal pride in his victory in *Brown v. Board of Education*.

Finally, I think a trickster lawyer's personal code should consider the issue of what I call psychological integrity. While we expressly recognize that misdirection and disingenuousness are important components of legal practice, we also have to face the fact that these professional virtues are often rightfully seen as vices in private life, where openness and transparency are highly valued.

There is a real danger that our professional mind-set will seep into our relationships in life beyond the office, or that the tension between appropriate conduct in different social arenas will exact a high psychological toll. Stories of "great" lawyers who are much less great spouses, parents, and friends are unfortunately common-place, as are statistics that lawyers rank highly in alcohol and drug abuse. Therefore, I think a trickster lawyer should work to be clever enough to make sure professional success does not destroy his or her private life.

For lawyers who choose to adopt it, the trickster identity should provide many psychological rewards. It emphasizes the creative nature of legal practice and the power that lawyers wield in shaping our economic, social, and political worlds. This creative power is not only gratifying in itself, but it also commands admiration and respect from the society at large.

I think the emphasis on creativity should be especially appealing to young lawyers, because creativity is a characteristic too seldom identified with the practice of law. Many students choose law school as a "safe" choice instead of following what they see as other more creative but less well-paid careers. They see the practice of law as requiring long hours of labor at routine tasks with little impact upon the public good. One benefit of the trickster identity is that it rejects the image of the lawyer as robotic scrivener or bloodless technician. Instead the trickster lawyer is a species of performance artist, continually reinventing the world we inhabit.

While the trickster identity shows promise in accentuating the creative aspect of legal practice, it also warns us of the danger that lawyerly cleverness might go too far, with deleterious consequences for both the society and the lawyer. Let's remember that the trickster identity does not create this problem. Lawyers will be cunning whether or not we call them tricksters, but the trickster identity does call attention to an aspect of legal practice that is seldom discussed. The technocrat lawyer may think he or she is only offering a service to customers who can pay, but the trickster lawyer knows that he or she is an active participant in creating the law, and therefore must take some responsibility for the product.[89]

The trickster identity celebrates the opportunities the practice of law creates, and at the same time it warns us of the ethical and psychological perils the practice of law presents. Would we expect anything less of a great profession?

About the Author

John Denvir has practiced and taught law for over forty years. His most recent book is *Freeing Speech: The Constitutional War over National Security* (2010).

John Denvir

Footnotes

[1] Joel Chandler Harris, *The Complete Tales of Uncle Remus* (Boston: Houghton Mifflin Company, 1955), 12.

[2] See Lewis Hyde, *Trickster Makes This World: Myth, Mischief, and Art* (New York: Farrar, Strauss and Giroux, 1998); Paul Radin, *The Trickster: A Study in American Indian Mythology* (New York: Schocken Books, 1972).

[3] I use the masculine because tricksters in mythology are always male.

[4] Hyde reprints the tale as Appendix I of *Trickster Makes This World*, 317–43.

[5] Hyde tells of a more direct challenge to the legitimacy of the old order in a Hindu tale about the trickster Krishna. Krishna likes to eat butter by the handful. When his mother reprimands him for the theft of the butter, he coolly replies, "I didn't steal the butter, Ma. How could I steal it? Doesn't everything in the house belong to us?" Hyde, *Trickster Makes This World*, 71.

[6] But the trickster is not always a hero. Often he shows himself to be amoral and sometimes foolish. His cocky confidence can get him into trouble. A good example of this is the Uncle Remus story of the "Tar-Baby," where Brer Rabbit's foolishness places him in the clutches of Brer Fox. See Harris, *Uncle Remus*, 6–9.

[7] Taylor Branch, *Parting the Waters: America in the King Years 1954–63* (New York: Simon & Schuster, 1988), 599. My discussion of King is based on this classic.

[8] Branch, 577.

[9] Branch, 631.

[10] Branch, 691.

[11] The following discussion relies on Allan M. Brandt, *The Cigarette Century: The Rise, Fall, and Deadly Persistence of the Product That Defined America* (New York: Basic Books, 2007).

[12] Brandt, 264.

[13] See Phillip N. Meyer, *Storytelling for Lawyers* (New York: Oxford University Press, 2014), esp. chap. 3. I rely on Meyer's analysis of Gerry Spence's final

summation to the jury. Eric E. Johnson has published a very helpful edited version of the argument at www.eejlaw.com/c/Silkwood_v._Kerr-McGee_T10.pdf.

[14] Meyer, *Storytelling for Lawyers,* 44.

[15] Meyer, 45.

[16] Meyer, 47.

[17] Meyer, 48.

[18] Meyer, 48.

[19] Meyer, 52-53.

[20] Eric Johnson, *Silkwood v. Kerr-McGee,* 12.

[21] Meyer, *Storytelling for Lawyers*, 52.

[22] Meyer, 55.

[23] Eric Johnson, *Silkwood v. Kerr-McGee*, 16.

[24] Plessy v. Ferguson, 163 U.S. 537 (1896).

[25] Brown v. Board of Education, 347 U.S. 483 (1954).

[26] Richard Kluger, *Simple Justice: The History of* Brown v. Board of Education *and Black America's Struggle for Equality* (New York: Alfred A. Knopf, 1975). The discussion in this section is based on Kluger's book.

[27] McLaurin v. Oklahoma State Regents, 339 U.S. 637 (1950).

[28] Kluger, *Simple Justice,* 267.

[29] Missouri ex. rel. Gaines v. Canada, 395 U.S. 337 (1938); *McLaurin*, 339 U.S. 637 (1950).

[30] Kluger, *Simple Justice,* 317.

[31] *Brown*, 347 U.S. at 494, fn. 11.

[32] Kluger, *Simple Justice,* 619.

[33] Kluger, 641.

[34] Kluger, 643.

[35] Kluger, 644.

[36] See Craig v. Boren, 429 U.S. 190 (1976); Romer v. Evans, 517 U.S. 120 (1996).

[37] This section relies primarily on Brooke A. Master's excellent book, *Spoiling for a Fight: The Rise of Eliot Spitzer* (New York: Henry Holt & Company, 2006).

[38] Master, 83.

[39] Master, 89.

[40] Master, 92.

[41] Master, 93.

[42] Master, 152.

[43] Ron Chernow, *Titan: The Life of John D. Rockefeller, Sr.* (New York: Random House, 1998), 225–27; Albert Z. Carr, *John D. Rockefeller's Secret Weapon* (New York: McGraw-Hill, 1962), 64–66.

[44] See Malcolm Gladwell, *Outliers: The Story of Success* (New York: Little, Brown and Company, 2008), 116–29, 154–58; Jeff Madrick, *Taking America: How We Got from the First Hostile Takeover to Megamergers, Corporate Raiding and Scandal* (New York: Bantam Books, (1987), 272–78.

[45] Moran v. Household International, Inc., 500 A.2d. 1346 (1985).

[46] See Bruce Allen Murphy, *Fortas: The Rise and Ruin of a Supreme Court Justice*, (New York: William Morrow and Company, 1988), 47–51; Robert Caro: *The Years of Lyndon Johnson: The Path to Power* (New York: Alfred A. Knopf, 1982), 369–85, 445–75.

[47] Caro, *The Years of Lyndon Johnson*, 369–85, 445–75.

[48] E.g., Karl Llewellyn, *The Common Law Tradition: Deciding Appeals* (Boston: Little, Brown and Company, 1960).

[49] Anthony G. Amsterdam and Jerome Bruner, *Minding the Law* (Cambridge: Harvard University Press, 2000), 35.

[50] See James B, White, *The Legal Imagination: Studies in the Nature of Legal Thought and Expression* (Boston: Little, Brown and Company, 1973), 802. "Is it then as simple as this: the narrative heart of every judicial opinion provides a way of controlling legal language by requiring the judge to talk two ways at once?"

[51] Amsterdam and Bruner, *Minding the Law*; White, *Legal Imagination*; Linda Edwards, *Once Upon a Time in the Law: Myth, Metaphor, and Authority*, 77 TENN. L. REV. 883 (2010).

[52] Marbury v. Madison, 5 U.S. 137 (1803).

[53] Jean Edward Smith, *John Marshall: Definer of a Nation* (New York: Henry Holt & Company, 1996).

[54] Smith, 12.

[55] Smith, 318.

[56] *Marbury*.

[57] *Marbury*, 176.

[58] *Marbury*, 176.

[59] *Marbury*, 176.

[60] Robert G. McCloskey, *The American Supreme Court*, 5th ed., ed. Sanford Levinson, (Chicago: University of Chicago Press, 2010), 27.

[61] McCloskey, 28.

[62] William Eskridge, *All About Words: Early Understandings of "Judicial Power" in Statutory Interpretation, 1776-1806*, 101 COLUM. L. REV. 900, 1071–72 (2001).

[63] Employment Division, Department of Human Resources of Oregon v. Smith, 494 U.S. 872 (1990).

[64] Sherbert v. Verner, 374 U.S. 398 (1963).

[65] See Thomas v. Review Bd. of Indiana Employment Div. 450 U.S. 707 (1981); Hobbie v. Unemployment Appeals Comm'n of Florida, 480 U.S. 136 (1987); United States v. Lee, 455 U.S. 252 (1982); Gillette v. United States; 401 U.S. 437 (1971); Wisconsin v. Yoder, 406 U.S. 205 (1972).

[66] My short biography of Scalia relies primarily on Joan Biskupic, *American Original: The Life and Constitution of Supreme Court Justice Antonin Scalia* (New York: Farrar, Strauss and Giroux, 2009).

[67] 494 U.S. 872 (1990).

[68] See cases cited in note 65.

[69] Antonin Scalia, *A Matter of Interpretation: Federal Courts and The Law*, ed. Amy Gutmann (Princeton: Princeton University Press, (1997), 8–9.

[70] *Smith*, 494 U.S. at 878–79.

[71] 455 U.S. 252 (1982).

[72] 406 U.S. 205 (1972).

[73] Goldman v. Weinberger, 475 U.S. 503 (1986).

[74] 450 U.S. 707 (1981).

[75] *Smith*, 494 U.S. at 885.

[76] *Smith*, 494 U.S. at 908 (Blackmun, J., dissenting).

[77] The exception, in my view, is his creation of a new category of "hybrid" free exercise/privacy cases. We don't require other plaintiffs to show that state action has violated to two provisions of the Constitution. Why should we demand it of free exercise claimants?

[78] See generally, John Denvir, *Freeing Speech: The Constitutional War over National Security* (New York: NYU Press, 2010), 2–5.

[79] Hyde, *Trickster Makes This World*, 20.

[80] Bush v. Gore, 511 U.S. 98 (2000).

[81] *Bush*, 511 U.S. at 109.

[82] Quoted in Alan M. Dershowitz, *Supreme Injustice: How the High Court Hijacked Election 2000* (Oxford University Press, 2002), 82.

[83] Margaret Jane Radin, "Can the Rule of Law Survive *Bush v. Gore*?" in *Bush v. Gore: The Question of Legitimacy*, ed. Bruce Ackerman (New Haven: Yale University Press, 2002), 117.

[84] See Biskupic, *American Original*, 248.

[85] See Deborah Rhode, *Access to Justice* (New York: Oxford University Press, 2006), 32.

[86] Rhode, 32

[87] Rhode, 34.

[88] Melanca Clark and Maggie Barron, *Foreclosures: A Crisis in Legal Representation* (NYU School of Law, 2009) available at http://www.brennancenter.org/sites/default/files/legacy/Justice/Foreclosure%20 Report/ForeclosuresReport.pdf.

[89] For an excellent discussion of the ethical dimensions of practice within the adversary system, see William H. Simon, *The Practice of Justice: A Theory of Lawyers' Ethics* (Cambridge: Harvard University Press, 1998).

www.ingramcontent.com/pod-product-compliance
Lightning Source LLC
Chambersburg PA
CBHW071237170526
45165CB00003B/1138